CONQUER YOUR FRIENDS IN CHESS

HOW TO PLAY CHESS FOR (ABSOLUTE) BEGINNERS

2nd Edition

BY MAXEN TARAFA

Chess: How to Play Chess for (Absolute) Beginners - 2nd Edition
Copyright © 2015 by Maxen Tarafa
All rights reserved. This book or any portion thereof
may not be reproduced or used in any manner whatsoever without the
express written permission of the publisher except for the use of brief
quotations in a book review.
www.theskillartistsguide.com

CONQUER YOUR FRIENDS IN CHESS

THE 4-IN-1 COLLECTION

Books in this collection:

1) Chess: **How to Play Chess** for (Absolute) Beginners……………….....4

2) Chess: Conquer your Friends with **8 Easy Principles**……………..125

3) Chess: Conquer your Friends with **4 Daredevil Openings**………188

4) Chess: Conquer your Friends with **10 Easy Checkmates**…………267

LETTER TO THE READER

Dear Reader,

Welcome to the 4-in-1 collection of the Conquer your Friends series. In this book, you will find a collection of four high-impact Chess books for beginners and post-beginners who want to learn fast.

In these books, I make a few big promises to my readers and I continue to keep them here: Easy-to-read, fun Chess books. No notation. No complex terminology.

After the astounding success of these four books, I figured it was time to combine them into one easy to find place.

In this book you will find the basics of Chess, including:
- How to set up the board
- The rules of the game and how to move the pieces
- Basic strategy
- Basic tactics
- Chess openings
- Endgame and checkmate patterns

These books have already changed the lives and games of thousands of players and if you read these books and practice the material, I promise you can greatly improve your game too.

Sincerely,

Maxen Tarafa

CONQUER YOUR FRIENDS IN CHESS

HOW TO PLAY CHESS FOR BEGINNERS

CHAPTER 1: HOW TO PLAY CHESS FOR (ABSOLUTE) BEGINNERS

My name is Maxen R. Tarafa, and I'm a Skill Artist.

If you're looking to learn a board game where you can tune out, roll some dice, and hope you're lucky enough to win, you've come to the wrong place.

But if you're looking for an ancient game of wits, war, and intellect, hop on your saddle partner. I'm going to show you how to play Chess at a beginner level in an alarmingly short amount of time.

Of course, a lot of books promise to teach the basics of Chess, but rarely deliver on results, so what makes this one different?

If you've read other Chess books for beginners, you may find a lot of interesting information…

…that you couldn't possibly learn from.

Many Chess books for beginners use a lot of complex terminology and strange symbols resembling the periodic table, such as **QxB6** and **NaH!?.**

If the symbols above look like a foreign language, you've come to the right place. You see, the problem with most books is they say they're for beginners, but they're actually NOT. They're written by Chess masters or internet marketers who don't realize beginners don't know how to read complicated Chess notation or terminology, and in my opinion, don't need to know.

My guess is you want to learn how to play Chess or refresh your knowledge on the basics, and you want to do it quickly and easily. Excellent.

While I'll take you through a more involved approach to learning Chess, I can promise that if you read this book and practice the recommended exercises, you will learn and (more importantly) remember the basics of Chess when you sit down to play, and do it faster than ever before.

Instead of dumping information on you, I want to lead you through a kind of guided meditation. To help you remember and understand, I'm going to ask you to stop and visualize, imagine, touch, move, and feel the Chess pieces and the moves at hand.

But, who am I? And why do I want to teach you how to play Chess so bad?

I grew up playing Chess against my brothers, cousins, and friends. In college, I started playing against my roommates, but I didn't win nearly as often as I would have liked. After I graduated from college, I wanted to get better at Chess, and found every bit of information I could find, and more than doubled my online rating from about 600 to 1300 in three months.

It wasn't until a while later when it came time to teach my nine-year-old brother Chess that I realized there were only a few easy principles that if the post-beginner just knew what they were and remembered them while playing, it would improve their game immensely. I taught him those principles and within a week he was beating 16 and 17-year-olds.

Later, after coaching a Chess club and continuing to improve my Chess game, I ended up writing a highly successful book called Chess: Conquer your Friends with 8 Easy Principles where I revealed the high impact principles I had taught to my younger brother and others.

Now, I want to apply the same philosophy to learning Chess for beginners: a focus on **remembering and using the information fast**, and not just reading it.

I've coached kids as young as 5 and adults as old as their thirties. I've taught everything from how to move a Pawn to how to avoid a Zugzwang. It doesn't matter how old you are or how little experience you have, if you promise to read this book carefully and practice the exercises, I promise you'll be confident at playing Chess at a beginner level in as little as a few hours.

After reading this book, you'll be well on your way to your own Chess empire, but remember with great power comes great responsibility.

I trust that you'll use it wisely.

Sincerely,

Maxen R. Tarafa

PREPARATION

If you own a Chess board, I highly suggest you take your Chess board out of the closet, dust it off, and take the pieces out.

In the first section, you're going to learn how to set up the board, the name of each piece, and how they move. Although I use copious images to help you along, people tend to learn best when they engage multiple senses. If you have a board, please feel free to touch, taste, smell, envision, hear, and even taste (if you feel so inclined) the piece we're covering.

If you don't have a Chess board and you're serious about learning Chess, you may want to consider buying one. You can often get a decent plastic one for less than $10 at any Wal-Mart, toy store, or online at Amazon. Although $10 or less is the cheapest, I recommend buying a wooden board in the $10 to $20 range because it will last longer, and you'll get more bang for your buck.

You can find an inexpensive wooden board I recommend here.

THE BEGINNER CHALLENGE

As a beginner, your greatest challenge is simply to remember these fundamentals. Rather than dump a lot of information on you, I'm going to walk you through each step like a guided meditation.

If you're an avid reader, you may be compelled to read the book as fast as you can. I suggest you don't. I'm going to instruct you on the best places to stop and visualize or try the exercises. Stop and imagine the piece and how it moves. Play with the pieces on the table and in your mind. You will gain the most from the book this way.

I'm going to have you pointing with your finger, counting out loud, and closing your eyes a lot so if you want to move to a place where people won't see you talking to yourself, you may want to move to new place now.

THE BOARD AND THE PLAYERS

In the **image below**, you see a complete Chess board. Most people have seen one before so I doubt it's a surprise. Let's talk about the board itself for a moment.

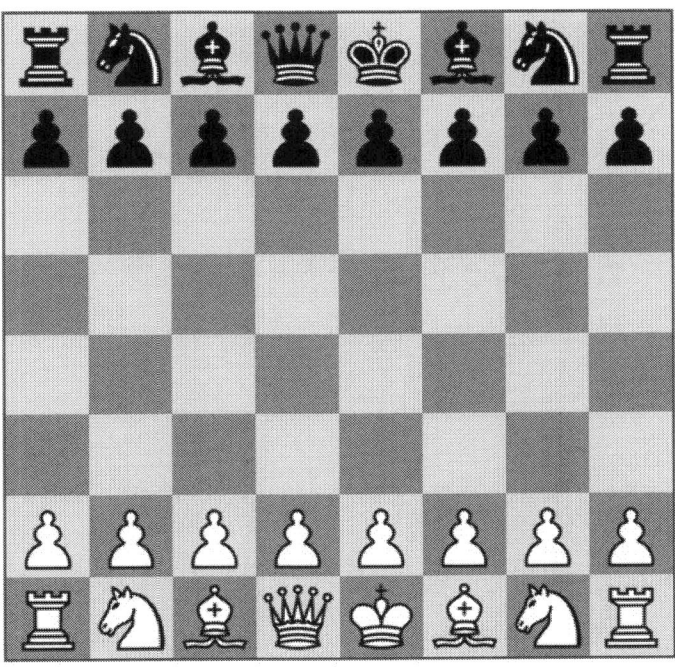

Every Chess board contains 64 alternating black and White squares. You may recognize that the Chess board looks exactly like a Checkers board (except some checkers boards are red and black).

There are two players and two sets of pieces. There are Black pieces and White pieces. The two players decide among themselves who is going to play White the other plays Black.

There are 16 White pieces and 16 Black Pieces and they are always set up exactly the same. It's important to note, **whoever plays White always moves first.**

After White makes the first move, Black moves, then White, then Black and so on. Each player alternates making one move at a time until the game ends. A player cannot make two moves on the same turn and cannot give up their move.

Board Orientation

While it may be intuitive for some, it's important I mention when I show an image of a board on the screen, such as in the **image above**, you can assume you are playing the role of pieces on the bottom (this simulates the pieces being closest to you.)

Next, I'll guide you through the names and abilities of each piece.

THE PAWN

The eight small pieces on each side are called Pawns. If you have the pieces in front of you, go ahead and pick this piece up now. If you don't, close your eyes and imagine you are picking up a Pawn.

The Pawn moves forward one square at a time. See the **image below**.

But, it can only capture diagonally forward one square. **See the image below**.

If you have a board, go ahead and set up the Pawns on the second row. First, try moving a Pawn one space forward. Then, set up a situation where the Pawn can capture another Pawn.

While the Pawn can only move one square at time, there is one exception. If a Pawn has not yet moved it can move two squares forward. However, this is the only time it can move two squares.

THE BISHOP

If you still have the Pawn in your hand, set it down and pick up the Bishop. Each player begins with two Bishops. Unlike the Pawn, there are no exceptions to how the Bishop moves.

The Bishop moves diagonally forwards or backwards. You'll notice if a Bishop is on a light square, it can only move to other light squares. If it's on a dark square it can only move to other dark squares.

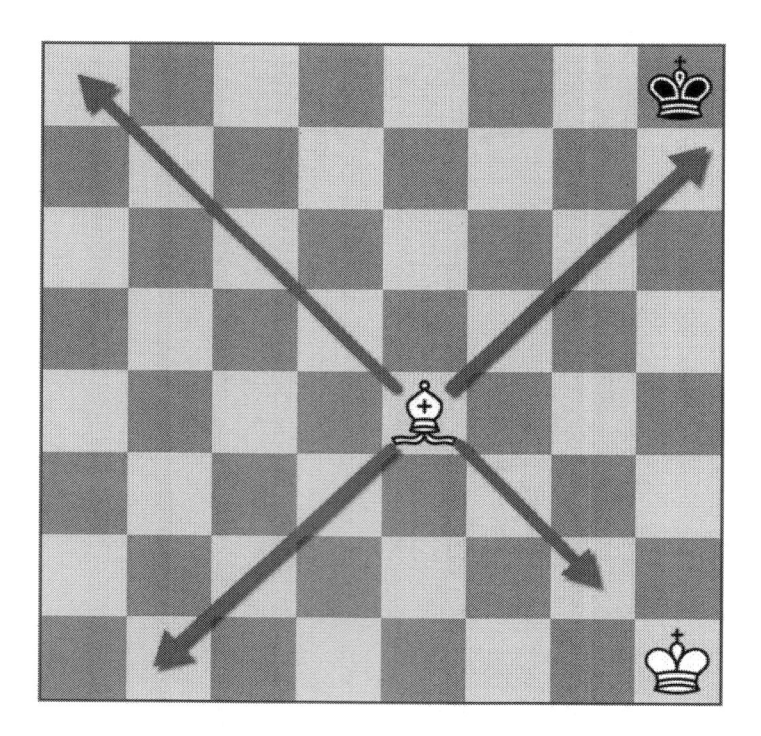

The way to remember how a Bishop moves is to recall the diagonal slit in the Bishop's "hat." **Diagonal slit** equals **Moves Diagonally.**

You can also think of its movements as an **"X"**.

Clear all the other pieces off the board and put two Bishops on it. One on a dark Square, one on a light Square. Try making 4 moves in each direction with each Bishop.

THE KNIGHT

The Knight is the trickiest piece on the board. It's difficult to remember how the Knight moves even for intermediate players so we're going to spend more time on the Knight than any other piece. Although the Knight is hard to learn, if you become good at using it, you'll have a massive edge on your opponents.

The Knight moves in an L-shape. Two squares in one direction, and one square perpendicular. It can move forward, backwards, or sideways. The Knight is also the only piece that can jump over other pieces!

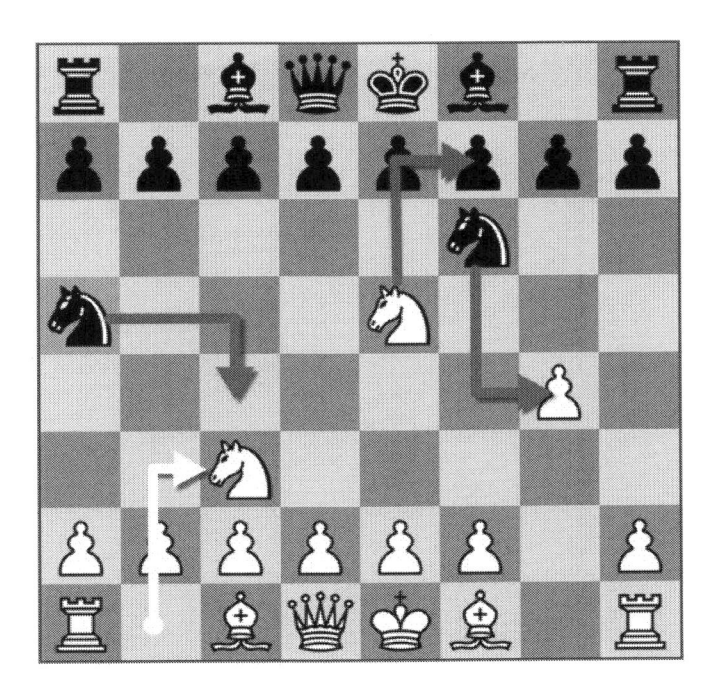

Yes, you heard that right. It can jump over your own pieces or your opponent's pieces. It captures opposing pieces by moving onto their square and removing that piece from the board.

Just to be clear, it doesn't capture an opposing piece by jumping over it like in Checkers. It only captures by moving onto an opposing piece's square.

The way it moves is quite tricky. Even experienced players struggle with predicting its movement. So, I'm going to show you how I remember how it moves. I call it the **One-Two-One Method**.

THE ONE-TWO-ONE METHOD

The One-Two-One Method helps me ensure I'm moving the piece to the right square. First, in the **image below**, you see the Knight moving in an L-shape.

I always count on the long side first. The long side is a distance of two squares from the square I'm already on. So, I count two squares. **One. Two.** Notice I don't count the square the Knight is currently on.

Then, I have to move one square in perpendicular or 90 degrees to the longside. In this instance, I'm going to go right. So, I count one square to the right. **One.**

Bam. I'm there.

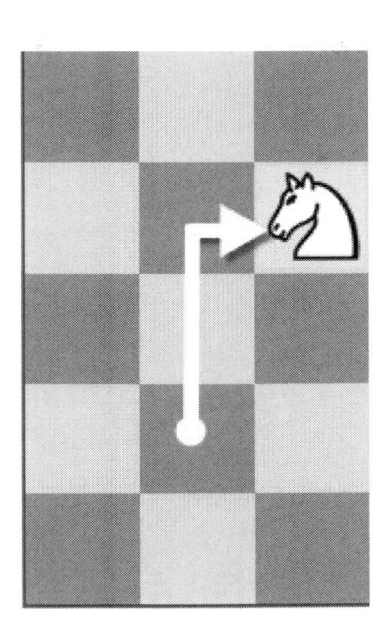

Let's review. Longside first. Two squares. **One two.** Then shortside 90 degrees one square. **One.**

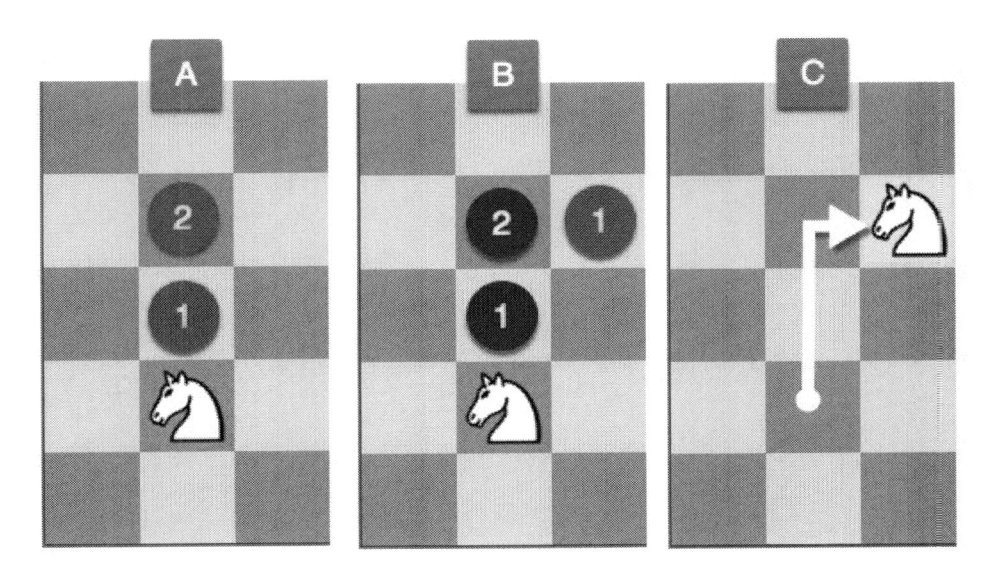

PRACTICE

Now try the **One-Two-One Method** on your own. Start your Knight anywhere on the board and move in an L-shape using the One-Two-One Method.

If you don't have a board in front of you, use the image above and point with your finger. Remember not to count the square you're already on.

Yes, you might look slightly like a fool pointing with your finger now, but when you're pulling Royal Forks and Discovered Checks with your Knight, your opponents won't be laughing.

Good. Now, try an exercise. Move your Knight from its original square to the square indicated with an 'X' in **the image below**. It should take you 4 moves.

It should look something like this:

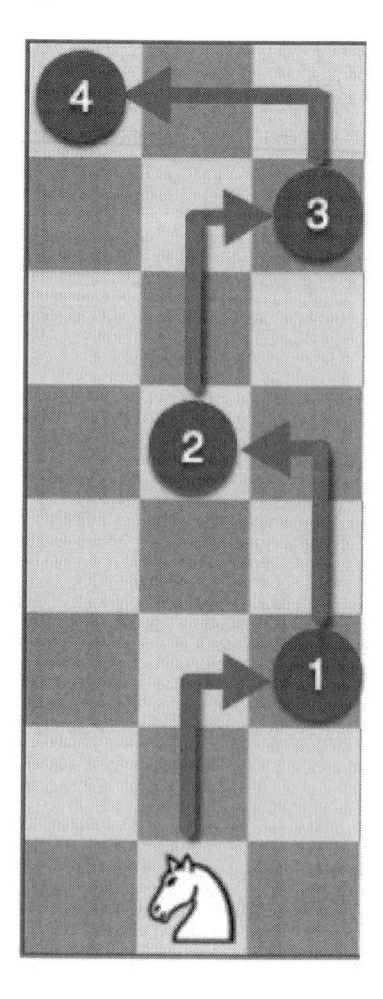

Great. The Knight is a complicated and tricky piece. But it's also the most useful. If you put your time into anything right now, put it into using the Knight.

If you skipped the Knight exercises above, GO BACK AND DO THEM! I promise it will be worth it. As you become more familiar with moving the pieces, you won't need to count out loud or point with your finger every time, but I promise doing it now will help you in the future immensely.

THE ROOK

The Rook is the second most powerful piece, and as the game continues and space grows on the board, the Rook becomes even more powerful.

The Rook moves left to right, forward and backward as many spaces as the board allows.

The Rook is also an important piece because it's a key piece in a special move called "Castling," which we'll cover after we talk about the King.

The way to remember how the Rook moves is to look at the top of it. On most pieces, there are four notches in the shape of a cross. The "Cross" will remind you the directions the Rook can move, horizontally and vertically.

QUEEN

The Queen is the most powerful piece on the board. She can move left to right, forward, backward, and diagonally in every direction as many squares as the board allows.

Although the Queen is very powerful, she's not invincible. It's not as hard as you might think to lose your Queen. You must be careful not to lose your Queen as she is your most powerful piece. Losing your Queen without a good reason will almost certainly lose you the game.

A common misconception about the Queen for beginners is that she can move to any square she wants. Although she can move in any direction, it doesn't mean she can jump over other pieces or move to a square that isn't directionally connected to the square she is on. When I say diagonal, vertical, or horizontal, it means in a straight line.

You can remember how the Queen moves because she typically has a circular crown on her head. The circular crown reminds you she can move in any direction.

THE KING

The King is the most valuable piece on the board because when the King is checkmated the game ends. He doesn't have a point value because you cannot capture a King. In this section, we're going to talk about how the King moves and captures.

Like the Queen, The King can move in any direction: left, right, forward, backward, and diagonal, but the King can only move a distance of **one square at a time.**

Like any other piece, the King can also capture pieces. If a piece is adjacent, he moves onto its square and removes it from the board.

It's easy to remember how a King moves because he's usually the heaviest and thickest piece on the board. I like to imagine his sheer size weighs him down and his weight only allows him to move one square at time.

CHECK, CHECKMATE, AND ILLEGAL MOVES

When you attack the enemy King, your opponent is in check and you must say "check." When *your* King is in check, you must remove your King from check in the next move.

The **image below** is an example of a King in check.

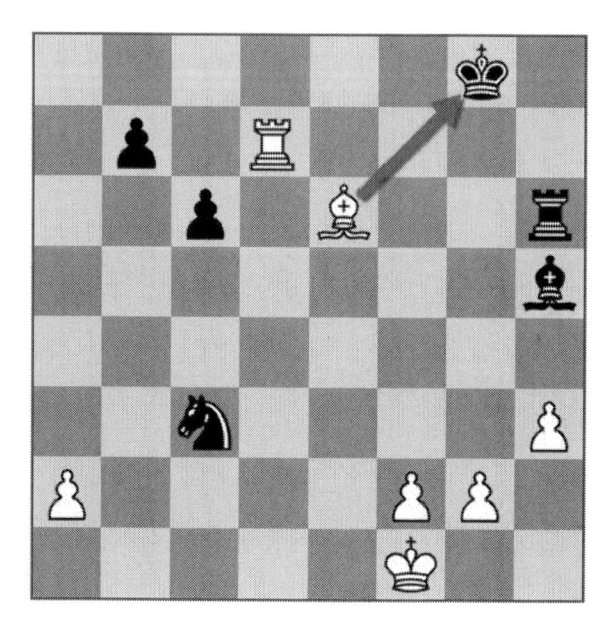

Your opponent can't capture your King, and you cannot choose to move another piece that doesn't take you out of check. If you made a move that didn't remove your King from check, you would have to take the move back and replay it. Similarly, you cannot make a move that puts your King *into* check. Such a move is illegal and again you would have to take the move back and replay it.

You can escape from check in a few ways.

1. **Move your King to another square where he's not in check.**

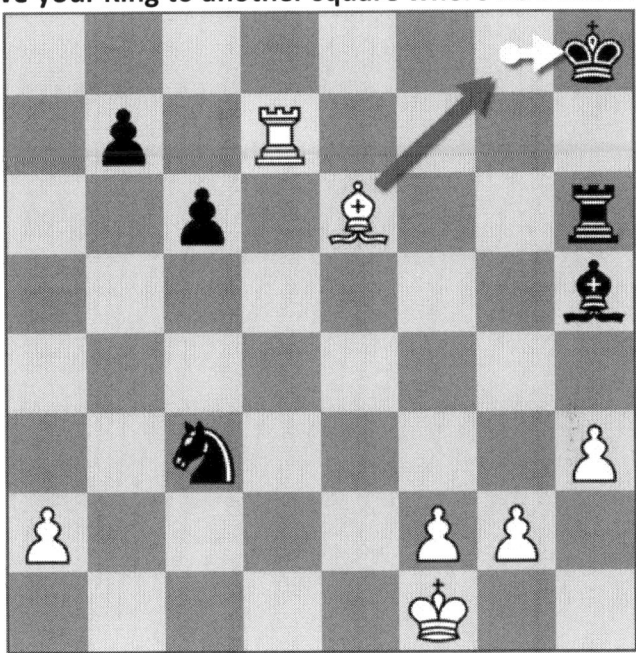

2. Move one of your pieces between your King and the piece that is checking you

3. Capture the piece checking you

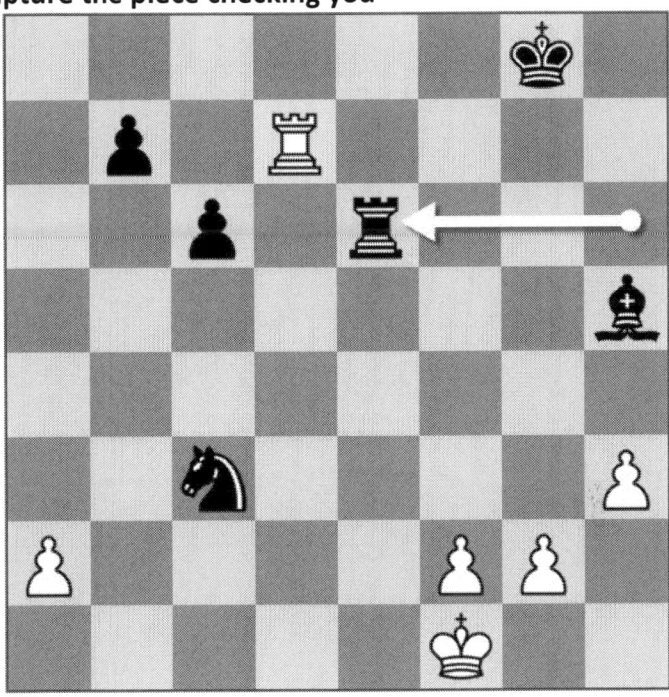

If your King is in check and you can't use any of the methods above to move your King out of check, it's **Checkmate**. The person whose King is checkmated loses and the game is over.

Checkmate is often a difficult concept for beginners, so let's examine it more closely.

In the **image below**, Black's King is in **Checkmate**. The White Bishop is checking him. Notice he cannot move to any of the other available squares because opposing pieces are attacking them all.

I've seen many beginners forget this, so I want to emphasize:

Once you're in checkmate, the game is over.

It doesn't matter how many pieces you or your opponent has. It doesn't matter how close you are to checkmating your opponent. If you're in checkmate the game ends right away.

I mention it because many beginners will checkmate their opponent, and not know what to do next. Then, they take the move back so their opponent can have space to escape. If you checkmate, you win! Now you can bask in the glory of winning!

REVIEW

Before we move on, let's review.

The Pawn can only move forward one square, except on its first move where it can move two squares. But, it only captures diagonally.

The Bishop moves diagonally forward, backward, left, or right as many squares as the board allows.

The Knight moves in an L-shape. It's easy to remember where the Knight moves using the **One-Two-One Method**.

The Rook moves left to right, forward and backward as many squares as the board allows.

The Queen can move left, right, forward, backward, and diagonally in all directions, and as many squares as the board allows.

The King can move in the same directions as the Queen. But, the King can only move one square at time.

GAMEPLAY REVIEW

The person playing White always moves first.

Check is when a player attacks the King, but the King can still escape. When a player is in check, he must move out of check immediately.

Checkmate is when a player's King is in check, and there is no way for his King to escape.

SPECIAL MOVES

There are three special moves in Chess: Castling, En Passant, and Promotion.

My younger brother literally cried the first time I castled against him. He didn't know the move existed, and he thought I was cheating. And I admit, if you'd never heard of it, it would definitely look like cheating. That's why I want to make sure you know about it from the beginning.

CASTLING

Castling is when a King and a Rook switch places in a single move. The King moves **two squares toward the Rook**, and the **Rook moves to the other side of the King**. It looks like this:

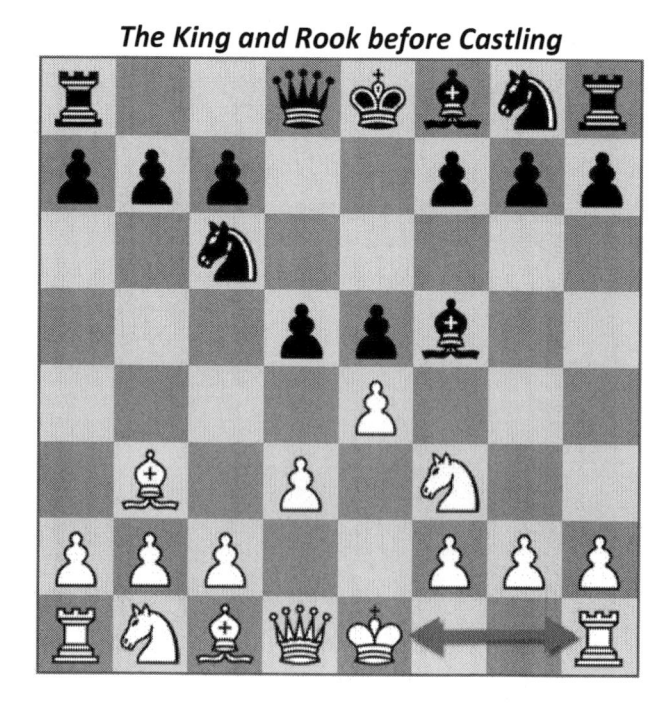

The King and Rook before Castling

The King and Rook after Castling

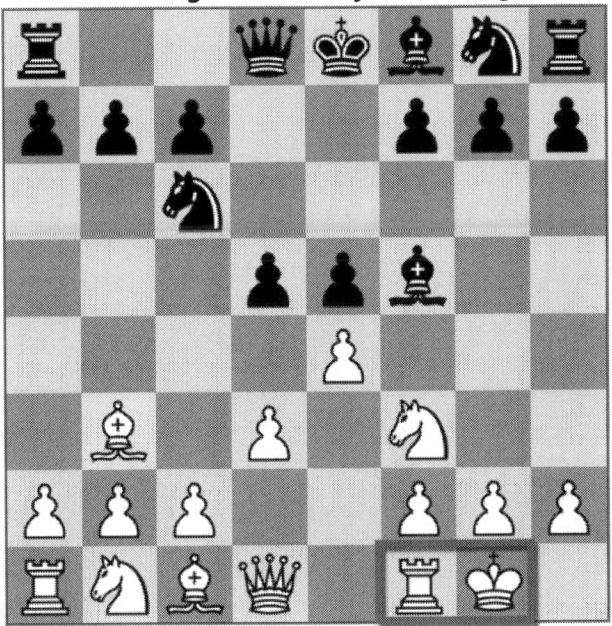

CASTLING RULES

There are a few rules that guide Castling, however. You can only castle if...

1. Neither the King nor the Rook, you plan to castle with has moved.

> Even if they've moved and then moved back onto their original squares, it's too late to castle.

2. There are no pieces between the King and the Rook

> Obviously this would make the old switcheroo difficult.

3. The King cannot castle from check, through check, or into check.

> This one's tricky. Since its illegal to put your own King into check, castling with a check in the equation isn't allowed. But let's break each part of this down...

THE KING CANNOT CASTLE FROM CHECK

If your King is currently in check (such as in the **image below)**, you can't castle. You must remove your King from check (without moving your King) and then castle.

THE KING CANNOT CASTLE THROUGH CHECK

If an enemy piece is attacking any of the squares between where your King is and where he's going after castling, you can't castle. See the **image below**. If you can block that piece or your opponent moves the piece, you can then castle.

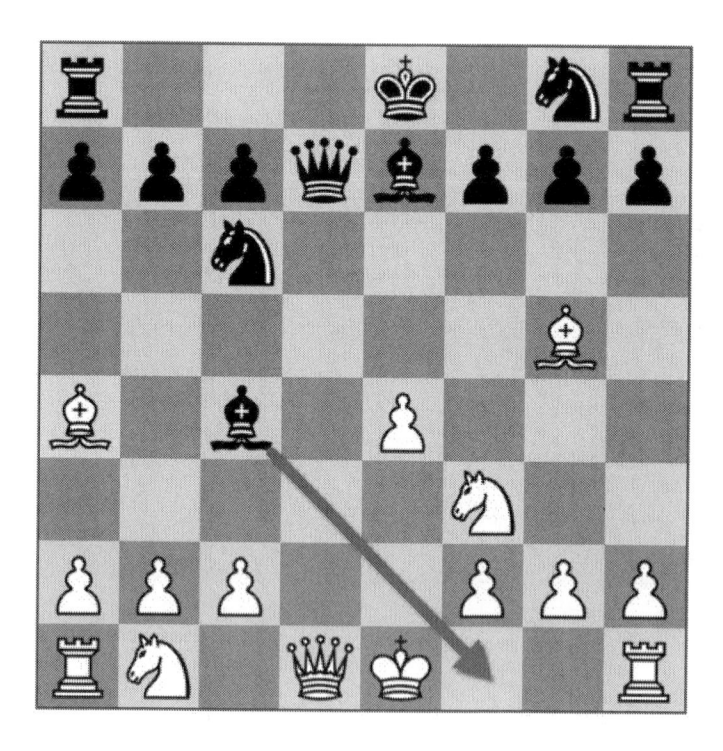

THE KING CANNOT CASTLE INTO CHECK

If your King will be in check on the square where he will be at the end of castling, you can't castle. This one is obvious since it's illegal to put yourself into check.

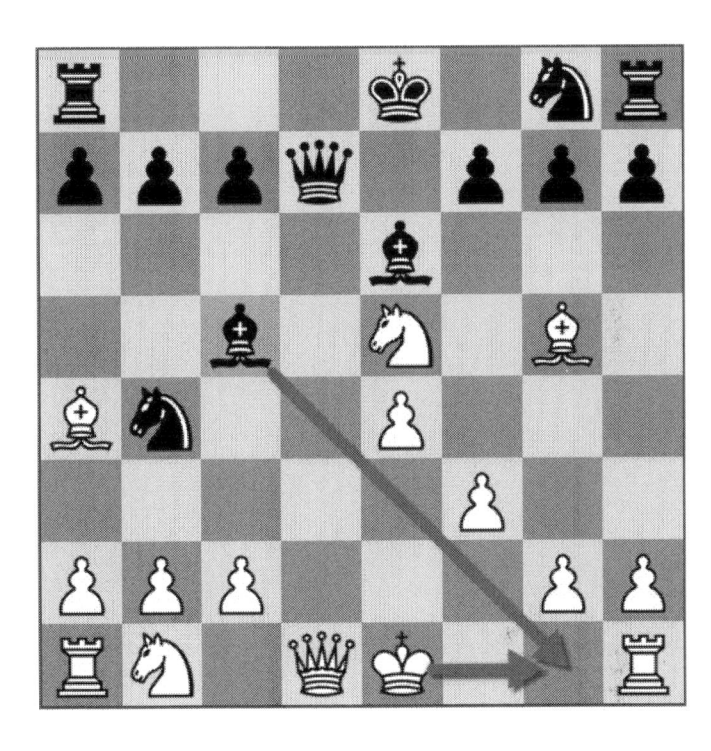

Other than that, you can castle anytime. Like I said, the main reason I'm telling you about this now is so you don't end up crying like my 9-year-old brother if someone suddenly pulls this on you. If you're interested in learning more about when and why to castle, check out the sequel to this book: Chess: Conquer your Friends with 8 Easy Principles where I explain it in more detail.

EN PASSANT

I'm not going to talk much about En Passant because it's rarely used in beginner games and it wouldn't have a huge impact if you wanted to use it. But En Passant is if an enemy Pawn is two squares away in the column beside you, and you move two squares on your first move, the enemy Pawn can take you as if you had moved only one square.

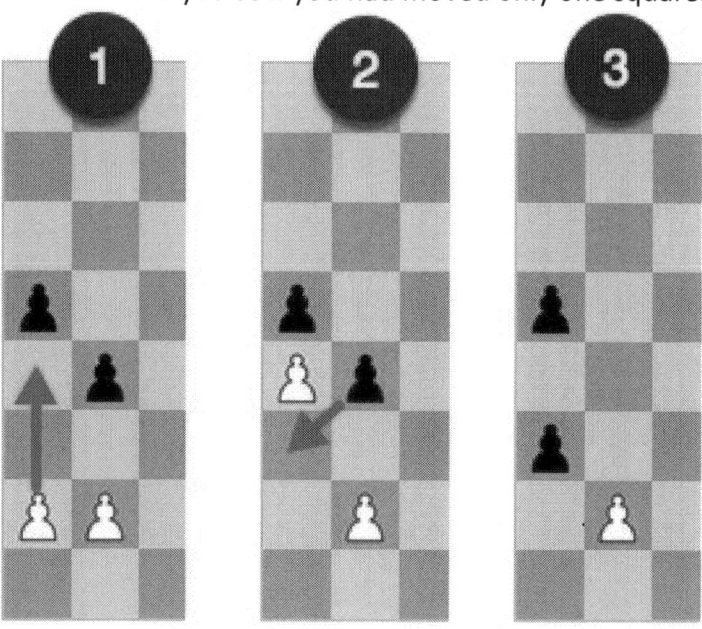

Like I said, it's rarely used, but it's good to know about.

PROMOTING

Promoting is extremely important, and if you remember any of the special moves, I suggest you remember this one. Because if you get into a game where most of the pieces are gone but there are still Pawns left, you may need to promote to finish the game.

Promoting is when you move a Pawn to the other end of the board, you can promote the Pawn to any piece you want other than a King or a Pawn. See the **image below**.

I've seen many beginners give up on a game with no winner because all their "good pieces" were gone, but they still had five Pawns on the board they could've Promoted to five Queens, but they didn't know what promoting was.

Below (on the left) is an example of a Pawn near the opposing side of the board. When the Pawn moves to the end (on the image to the right) the Pawn can promote to a Queen.

HOW TO SETUP THE BOARD

Now that you're familiar with the pieces, how they move, and how to win the game, let's go back to the beginning. How do you setup the board, and how do you remember where each of the pieces goes without referencing this book or searching Google? If you have a board in front of you, clear the pieces off and let's set it up together.

First, you want to make sure the board is oriented the right way. You can tell if the board is in the right direction if the square on your close right-hand corner is White. Here's a phrase to help you remember it: **"White on the Right."**

If you have a Chess board in front of you, go ahead and touch the White square in the lower right-hand corner now. If you don't have one, point with your finger at the corresponding square on the screen.

46

Next, set up your King and Queen. How do you know which goes on what square? Here's a way to remember it: "**Queen on her Color.**"

For example, if you're playing White, the White Queen goes on the central White square. The Black Queen goes on the central Black square.

You can check if it's done right by seeing if the Queens are directly across from each other. If they are, they're set up correctly. See the **image below**.

If you have a board, go ahead place your Queen on her color now. If you don't have a board, point your finger at the square where the White Queen would go.

47

Next, the Pawns are the easiest to remember. They all go in the second row. They're the front lines in your Chess army.

Set the Pawns on the board now.

Next, I usually place my Bishops. The way I remember where the Bishops go is because in Medieval times, the church and the throne often worked hand in hand, so the two Bishops go on either side of the King and Queen. The Bishops are also the second tallest pieces, so it's easy to think of them sitting next to the royalty.

The Knights are between the Bishop and the Rook. I usually imagine a Knight on a horse standing in front of the drawbridge of a castle. This reminds me that only the Knight is next to the Rook.

Go ahead and set your Knight pieces now.

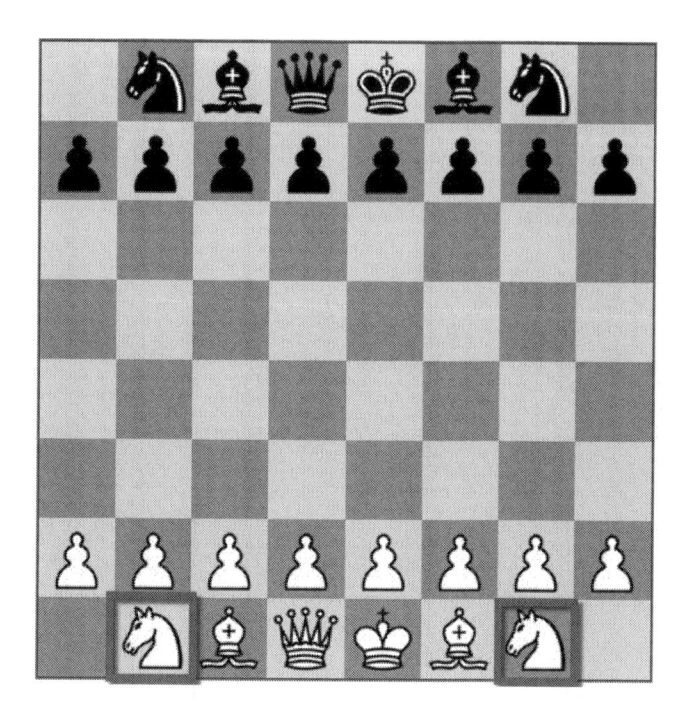

Then I place my Rooks. The Rooks look like castles. So, I like to think the Kings, Queens, Bishops, and Knights live inside the castle. So, the castle-shaped pieces enclose them.

Finish the set up and place the Rooks in the correct position now.

That's it. You're done! It's important to remember to set up the board, exactly the same every time. If you set up the board incorrectly, and don't realize it until you're several moves into the game, you may have to start over.

The main things to remember from this exercise is **White on the Right**, and **Queen on her color**, and the rest will fall into place.

PRACTICE, PRACTICE, PRACTICE

Now you know how to play Chess. I suggest you now find a friend who wants to learn Chess or knows how to play and play at least five games.

If you don't have anyone to play against, you can play on a Chess program. Most computers come installed with a Chess program where you can play against a computer. Or, you can go online and find online programs. My favorite Chess website is Chess.com. You can play Chess against random opponents who are at your level, or you can play digitally against your friends.

You can also download an app for your phone. The app I use is called Chess with Friends (made by the same people as Words with Friends). This is a great way to play against random people, but you never know how good they are.

I cannot emphasize enough how important it is to play the game. You simply can't expect to remember what you've learned without practicing.

In the next section we're going to talk about strategy. If you've never played Chess before I still suggest you play a few games before moving on to the next section. If you're just refreshing what you already know, you'll probably be ready.

BASIC STRATEGY AND OBJECTIVES

Strategy is a little beyond the fundamentals. For most absolute beginners, I would recommend practicing how to move the pieces and playing a few games. But, in this section, I want to leave you with some basic tips and strategies for chess.

In Chess, you have one fundamental objective: checkmate your opponent. But checkmating your opponent is easier said than done. So, there's another objective you're more likely to achieve first.

You take your opponent's pieces.

For example, if you have a King, a Queen, a Bishop, and a Rook, and your opponent only has a King and a Pawn. You're much more likely to win because you have more pieces.

So, the basic strategy is to take your opponent's pieces until your pieces outnumber his or hers and you are strong enough to checkmate.

However, taking your opponent's pieces (or material as it's often called) isn't everything.

At different times of the game, you may want to turn your focus to other goals, which brings me to...

THE THREE PHASES OF A CHESS GAME

Every Chess game has three basic phases. The Opening, The Middle Game, and the Endgame. At each phase of the game your focus shifts to a different element.

OPENING

The opening is approximately the first 10 moves of the game. In the opening, your focus is to **Develop your Pieces** and **Control the Center**.

Developing your pieces means moving your pieces out. You want to involve as many pieces as you can as early as possible. Many beginners (often remembering Checkers) only move their Pawns forward in the opening. This is a mistake in Chess. You want to use a combination of your Pawns, Bishops and Knights in the Opening to control the center of the board.

The **image below** shows you the center. If your opponent is any good, he won't let you have full control of the center. Controlling the center is a challenge for every level of player, but the basic idea is to move your pieces toward this area, and it will be harder for your opponent to attack you.

Opening Tip

The best tip I can give absolute beginners in the opening is to move move your King Pawn first (see the image below). A King Pawn move also works well when you're playing Black. This will give you the most options for development and will help to control the center.

Once you've gotten used to Chess gameplay, you can start learning more openings, but this first move will be a great start.

If you want to learn more about Opening techniques, check out my book Chess: Conquer your Friends with 4 Daredevil Openings, where I cover opening principles in more detail. You'll also get 4 of the openings I personally use and that I believe are the most effective for casual players and beginners. By the way, an opening is a move-by-move plan for your first 5 to 10 moves.

In this edition, I've also included a free mini-book download that lists the top 6 moves NOT to make in the Opening. By simply not making these 6 moves you will have improved your game dramatically. You'll find the link and a description at the end of the book.

THE MIDDLE GAME

If you played the opening right, your pieces should be developed by the Middle Game. Although you're still maintaining control of the center a little, you're now shifting your focus toward taking your opponent's pieces and breaking the barriers to your opponent's King for checkmate.

For example, a middle game could look something like this...

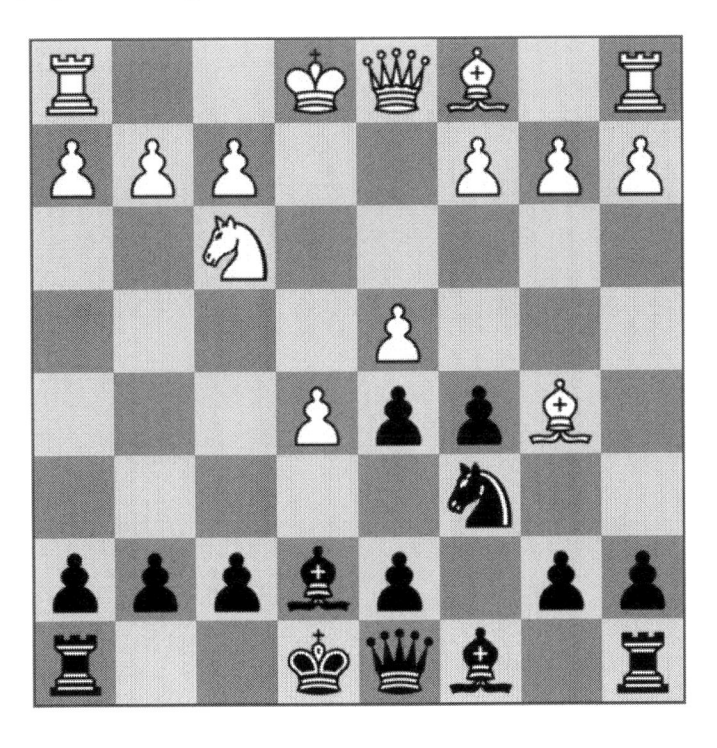

The basic idea is to take your opponent's pieces without losing your own. Mindblowing concept, right? But it's easier said than done.

Let's try it. In the image above, there's a loose piece that Black can take in two moves. Can you guess which piece it is?

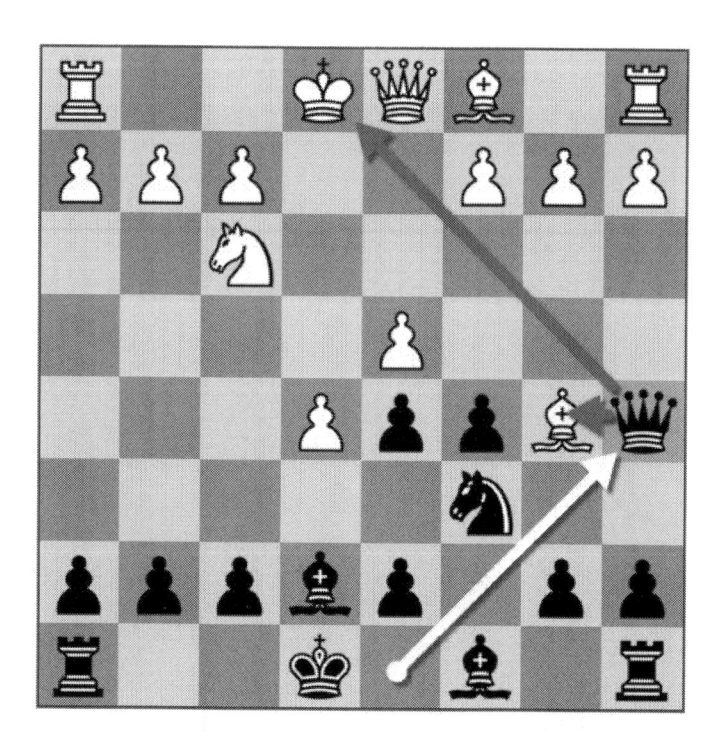

In the image above, you can see that if Black moves the Queen diagonally, he can attack both the King and the Bishop at the same time.

Since White must get the King out of check, he blocks the Queen's attack with the Bishop….

But that means…..

Black can take a free piece!

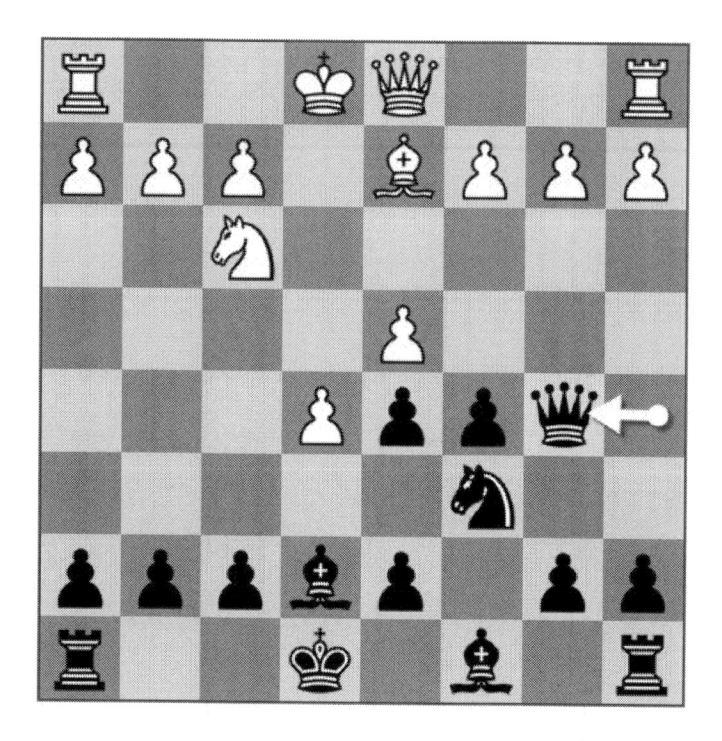

Now Black gets to take a free piece without losing one of his own.

Taking your opponent's pieces relies on **Chess Tactics**. Tactics are like mini-strategies to take your opponent's pieces, which often involves one of your pieces attacking two enemy pieces at the same time.

There are many different types of tactics and it would take a long time to explain them all. But, the basic idea is try to take your opponent's pieces without losing yours.

THE ENDGAME

In the endgame, you're finding a way to checkmate your opponent. There are probably less pieces on the board, and you're probably fighting to align all your pieces towards your opponent's King.

Checkmate can be confusing for absolute beginners so I want to show you some examples.

Example #1 Queen and Rook

Here's an example of a common beginner checkmate with a Queen and Rook.

Do you see the checkmate?

Here's the same board, but this time with arrows showing how White's Queen, Rook, and even King work together to checkmate Black's King.

Notice that White's Rook is blocking Black's King from the rest of the board. The White Queen delivers the checkmating blow.

The Queen and the Rook are two of the best pieces for checkmating in the endgame. If you play right, they're also the most likely to survive to the end.

Example #2 Queen and Bishop

In the checkmate below, White's Queen checkmates with the support of the Bishop. The arrow below shows how the Bishop supports the Queen.

Since the Bishop is supporting the Queen, Black's King cannot capture it. Remember that since a King cannot move into check, he cannot capture a piece if it would put him in check. So, capturing the Queen here would be illegal.

And since Black can't move right, left or to any other adjacent squares, he is in checkmate.

In the endgame, you must use all your available pieces to corner your opponent's King and put him into checkmate.

Endgame Tip

If I could give one tip for the endgame, it's to use your strongest pieces (like your Queen or your Rook) to slowly move the opposing King into a side or a corner, and then use another piece to checkmate him. It almost always takes two pieces to checkmate.

And don't forget your King can help too!

There is an art to checkmate and there's much much more to learn. That's why I compiled an entire book of checkmates in *Chess: Conquer Your Friends with 10 Deadly Checkmates*. *10 Deadly Checkmates* is for somewhat advanced beginners, but you can easily catch up by practicing what you learn here and practicing.

STRATEGY CONCLUSION

If you're interested in learning more strategy, check out my book <u>Chess: Conquer your Friends with 8 Easy Principles.</u> In this book, I cover 8 of the highest impact principles that can help you improve your Chess game. I originally wrote it for people who have played for years but didn't know any strategy, but if you learn and practice the techniques in this book, you'll be ready for it.

While strategy can be useful for beginners, most beginners don't lose because their strategy or tactics aren't up to speed. More often it's because they have trouble perceiving that pieces are in danger or they don't think ahead far enough to know that they will lose a piece a few moves ahead. In the next section, you'll learn how to address these common visual game problems.

Again, if you've never played Chess before you may want to play a few games before moving on to the next section. If you're stubborn, and a voracious information-fiend like I am, you're probably going to read it anyway. So, I recommend playing a few games afterward and coming back to re-read the next section when it will make more sense.

VISUAL GAME

THE VISUAL GAME FOR BEGINNERS

Although you typically see players moving pieces, most people don't think about what's going on behind the curtains...the curtains of the mind, that is. In order to win a Chess game, you also need to have strong visual Chess Game.

When I say Visual Chess Game, I mean visualization and calculation that takes place in your head or your mind's eye.

Most books won't show you this, but you need to have a strong grasp of what's going on inside your head in order to win. Someone with strong visual game can beat someone without the knowledge of tactics and strategy, but someone with knowledge of tactics and strategy with bad visual game cannot do the reverse.

VISUALIZING ACTIVE PIECES

In order to win a Chess game, it's not quite enough to see the pieces as they are on the board. You must also be able use your mind's eye to predict opportunities and dangers for your pieces and those of your opponent's. In this exercise, we're going to gain a basic ability to visualize the active pieces on the board.

Let's say you want to move your Bishop. In order to find a safe square to move your Bishop to, you must first visualize the active pieces on the board.

In the **image below**, you're playing White and it's your turn. Your Bishop has an easy move that can take another piece in 1 move. Can you visualize an arrow with your mind's eye that will lead to the Bishop highlighted below taking an opponent's piece? If it helps, draw a line with your finger from the highlighted Bishop to the active piece.

67

If you visualized a direct line from the White Bishop to the Black Bishop, you're correct.

See the **image below**.

Every time it's your turn to move, you want to visualize if you can take an opponent's piece.

Obviously, if you have an opportunity to take an opponent's piece without any negative consequences, you should. But in order to see that you have an opportunity in the first place, you must actively visualize in your head where your pieces can move and more importantly if they can move to a square that takes an opponent's piece.

As you become better, you can visualize these arrows without pointing with your finger. But I promise you will learn faster if you start by pointing first.

Let's try another example, in the **image below** the highlighted Rook has an opportunity to take an opposing piece, can you visualize the line from the Rook to the opposing piece?

69

If you visualized a line between the Rook and the Black Knight, you visualized correctly. See the **image below.**

Okay, those were easy. Let's try a harder one. In the **image below**, there's a Bishop that can take another piece in one move. Find the Bishop, then visualize it taking the enemy piece. Only move to the next page when you're ready for the answer.

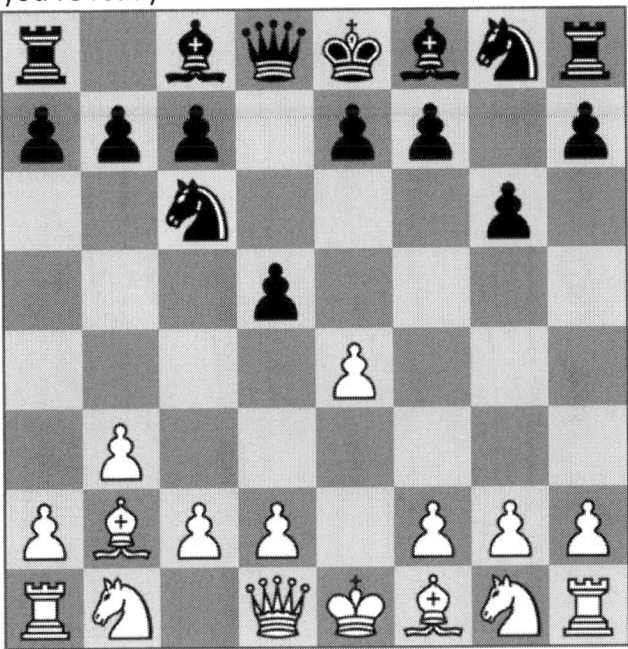

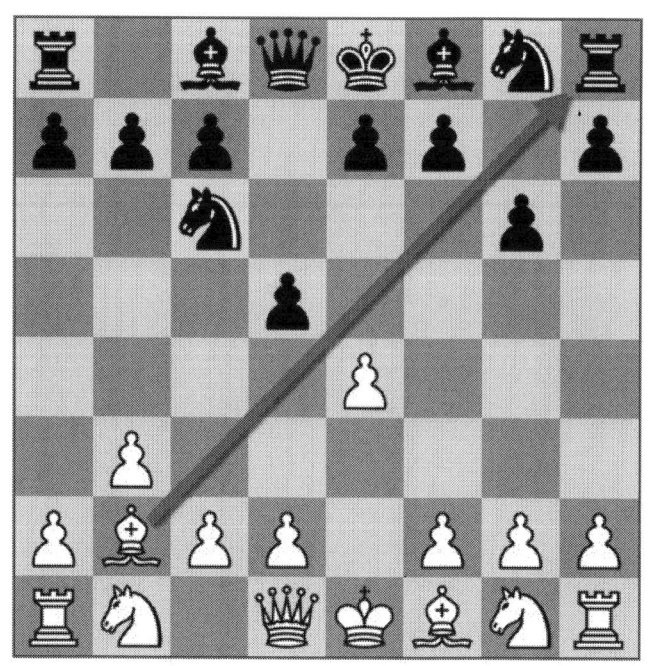

In Chess lingo, one would say the Bishop pointing toward the Rook in the opposite corner is fianchettoed. To fianchetto a Bishop is to move it toward the flank so as to command the long diagonal to the other side of the board. Many beginners will fail to see an enemy Bishop in this position, resulting in a loss of their Rook.

If you saw this move in a real game, you'll be winning by a lot.

ACTIVE VS. INACTIVE PIECES

Now you know how to visualize attacking lines between two pieces. But let's take a moment to point out the difference between active pieces vs. inactive pieces.

For the purposes of these lessons, an active piece is any piece that can have an immediate impact on the game. It's not always easy to determine which pieces are active and which aren't. It's more of an art than a science, but this is part of the challenge of playing Chess.

In the **image below** you see the board if you visualized where every single piece *can* move.

Too much, right? If you visualized where every piece *can* move, it would be very difficult to decide which piece to move next and what your most important priorities are. That's why you have to decide which pieces are the most active and visualize only those pieces.

Here's the **same image below,** but this time we're recognizing the Black King is in check, so clearly the Rook checking him and the Black King are inactive. White's dark-square Bishop is also hanging. Hanging means that it's unprotected and an enemy piece can take it in one move. The Black Rook will take the Bishop in the next available move...*if* we don't do something about it. So, after Black moves his King out of check, White must next move his Bishop out of the way or it will be taken.

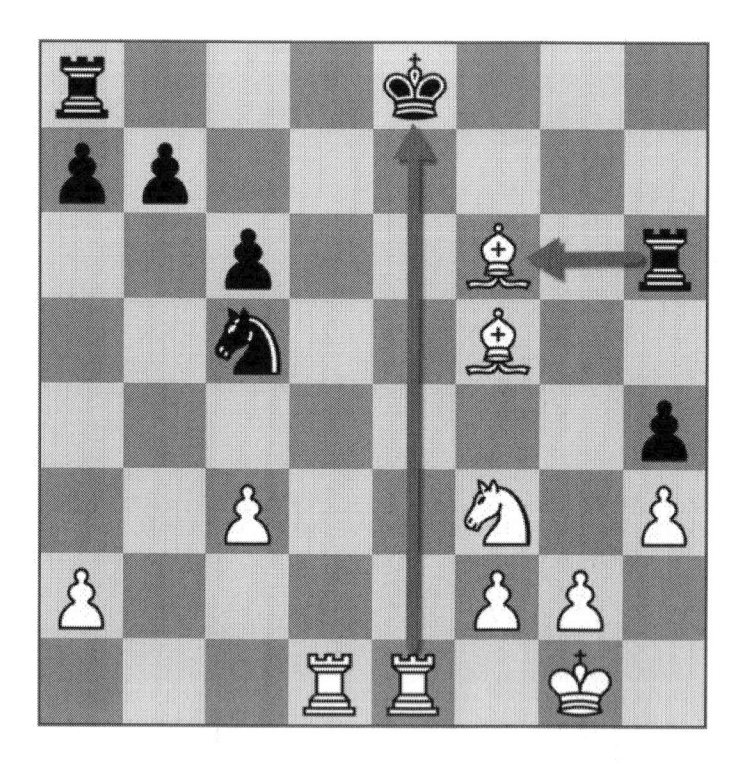

How do you decide if a piece is active or not? Couldn't all pieces potentially be active?

Ideally, all your pieces *would* be involved in the strategy you're pursuing, but this is rarely the case. I usually consider a piece inactive, if it takes 2 or more moves to affect me or my opponent's strategy. At the point where it can affect the game in one move, is when I would consider it active.

However, you could layer the active status of pieces further. In the **image below,** I would consider the highlighted pieces the next most active. The other pieces that don't have arrows to or from them, I would call inactive since it would take much longer for them to actively impact the game.

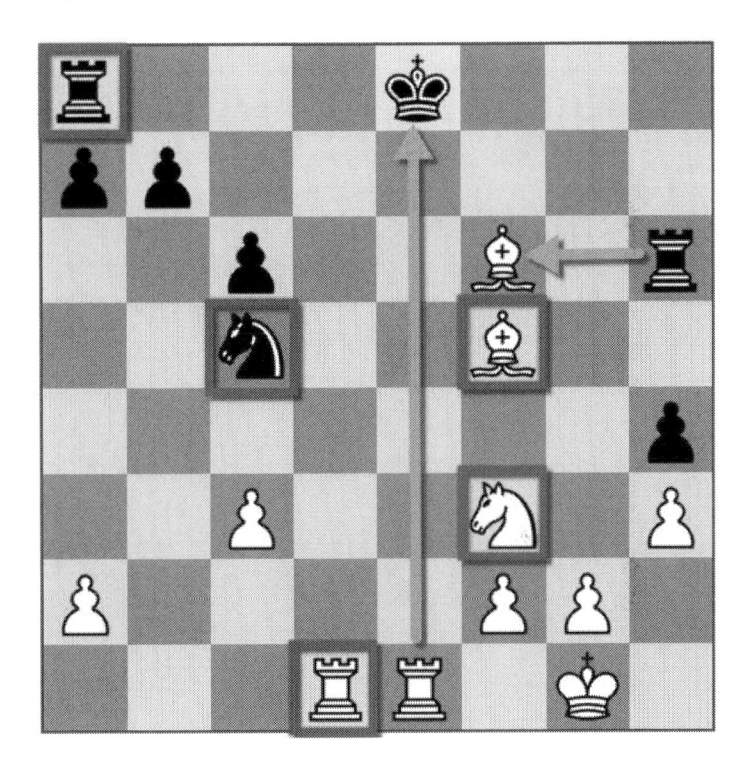

It's not always easy to decide which pieces are active and which aren't. This is part of your decision-making and creativity.

PREDICTING YOUR OPPONENT'S INTENTIONS

Now you know how to visualize when your pieces can attack another piece and roughly how to decide which pieces are active. But there's another side to the game, and that's your opponent's moves. You must also recognize and visualize when your opponent has the ability to attack *you*.

We can safely assume that your opponent wants the same thing you want….to win the game. At the beginner level, your opponent will have two main motivations: to take your pieces or checkmate you.

Every time your opponent moves, we can assume your opponent is trying to do one of those two things. So, every time your opponent moves, you must also visualize your opponent's active pieces.

For example, in the **following image,** Black has just developed the Bishop highlighted. Visualize the highlighted piece. What do you think Black is trying to do with his Bishop?

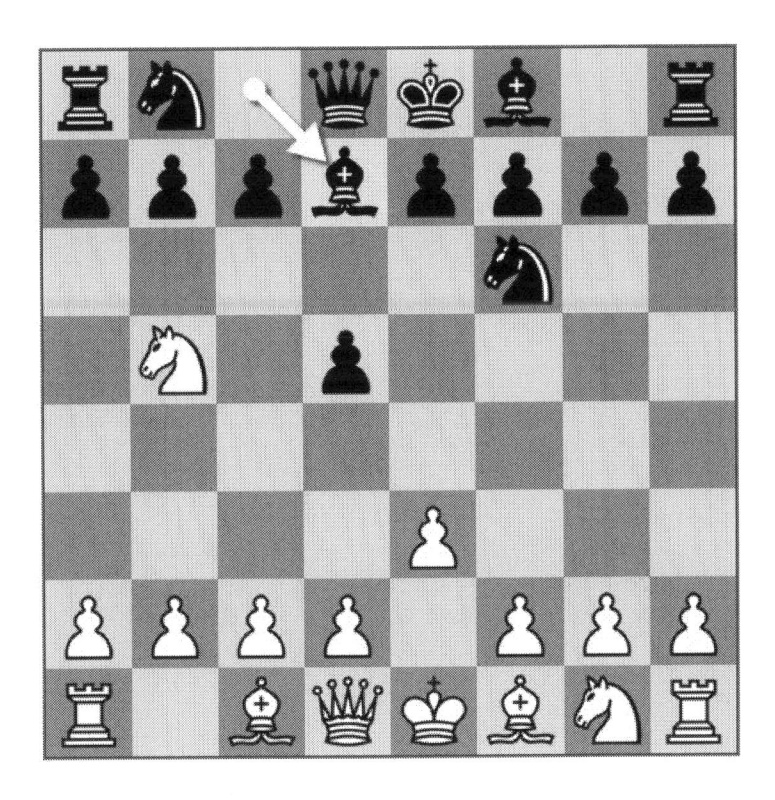

If you predicted Black was trying to attack your White Knight. You're correct. See the **following image**.

77

Every time your opponent moves, you must visualize and predict their moves as if you were playing your opponent's pieces. I typically ask myself, "if I was playing my opponent's pieces, what would my best move be?" You want to predict the best moves your opponent can make so you can be prepared for them before they happen. In general, you don't want to assume your opponent won't see good moves. Prepare for them to make the best moves they can.

BASIC MENTAL CHECKLIST

Making mistakes is easy, especially in Chess where there are a lot of decisions to make. It was Shakespeare or some famous philosopher who said "to err is human." And I believe it. But, we can avoid silly mistakes in Chess, by employing a **Mental Checklist** before every move.

Checklists are very popular with engineers and medical personnel because they ensure simple tasks that need to be done *are* done and not forgotten. Now, after seeing the effectiveness of checklists, many other industries and self-improvement gurus are using them, and now I do too.

Now, many "experts" and experienced players will say, running through a checklist when you play is not necessary and it's intuitive, but I guarantee anyone who has actively improved their Chess started with some form of a mental checklist until they became used to it and now they do it intuitively.

As you become more experienced and you start playing faster, your checklist will become more intuitive as well.

First, before you make a move you want to make sure you're not putting the piece you want to move in danger. You want to visualize the square you want to move to and then visualize the active enemy pieces. If they can take you with no consequences, you don't want to move there. So, first ask yourself **"Can any enemy pieces immediately capture my piece if I moved it to this square?**

This may seem obvious to some people, but you'd be surprised how often beginners and even intermediate players move to squares where they'll lose the piece for no good reason.

Next, you'll want to ask yourself...will this move put one of my other pieces in danger? Many times, moving one piece to a square better for your attack, removes a piece from your defense. Before you move to a square, ask yourself, **"Will moving this piece here affect the defense of my other pieces?"**

The top two questions are the most important. I encourage you to start with those two. As you play more games, there's one more question I would encourage you to ask yourself before you move: **"Can an enemy piece force me to move back?"**

When you make moves that force you to take back the move you just made you lose what Chess players call tempo, or in other words, you lose piece development. Your opponent gets to make moves that advance toward yours, but *your* pieces only move back.

So, here's the checklist I recommend below.

1. Can any enemy pieces immediately capture my piece if I moved it to this square?

2. Will moving this piece here affect the defense of my other pieces?

3. Can an enemy piece force me to move back? (optional)

This is a checklist for absolute beginners, but it can be used at any stage of the game. As you learn more, you will add to this checklist. But for now, ask yourself these questions before you move.

THINKING THREE MOVES AHEAD

In Chess, perception is the name of the game. But it's not only about perceiving the moves already on the board. You must also be able to predict and plan moves in advance. This can be an intimidating idea for beginners, but I promise the more you play the easier it becomes. You may already be thinking further ahead than you think. In this section, I'm going to show you how to see three moves ahead.

If you are visualizing the active pieces as they are on the board, you're probably already thinking two moves ahead. Congratulations! You're already two thirds of the way there. Now we're going to examine that third visualization that will put you one more step ahead of your opponent.

Let's take the Bishop example from above. But let's say there's another piece that factors into it. Let's say there's a Knight protecting the square where you want to move. **See the image below.**

We already know if we move to the square indicated in the **image below**, we can **predict the enemy Bishop will take our Bishop**. BUT, there's another factor to this equation. Do you see the White-squared Bishop that can also move to that square?

The exchange below involves our Knight, the Black Bishop, and the White Bishop, and the exchange will take three moves. Let's go step-by-step through how the next three moves will take place if we move our Knight as indicated below.

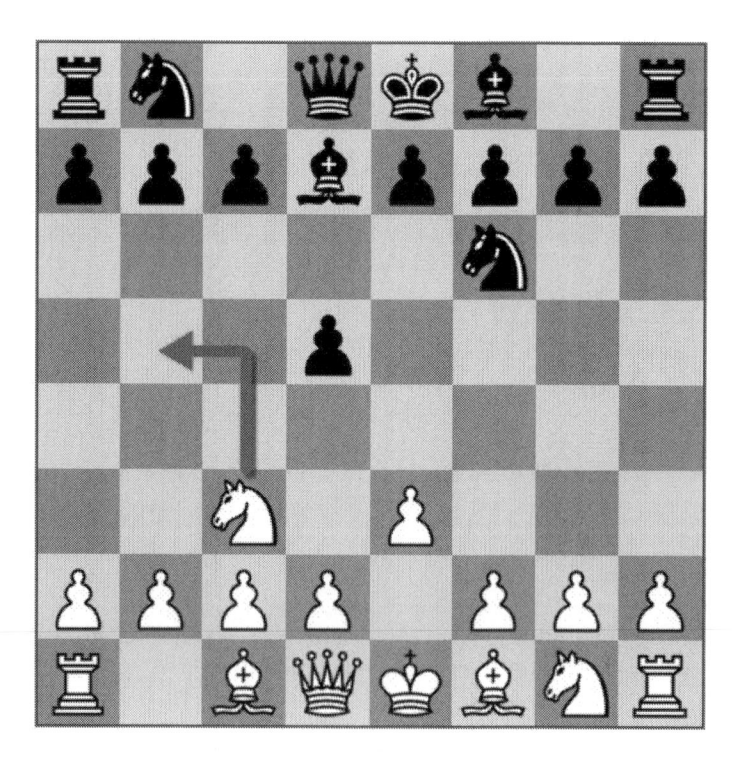

In the **image below**, we see the Knight moved to our desired square. We can count this as move **number one**. So, what happens next?

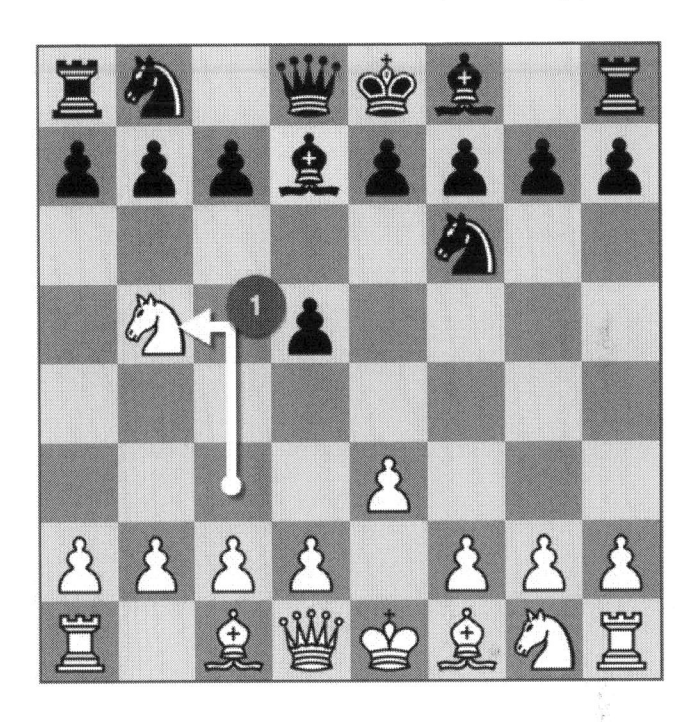

In this case, we're going to predict the Black Bishop will take our Bishop. Do we know for certain Black will make this move? No. But, we must visualize how the exchange will end up, if he does.

In move **number 2**, the Black Bishop takes our Knight. Then what?

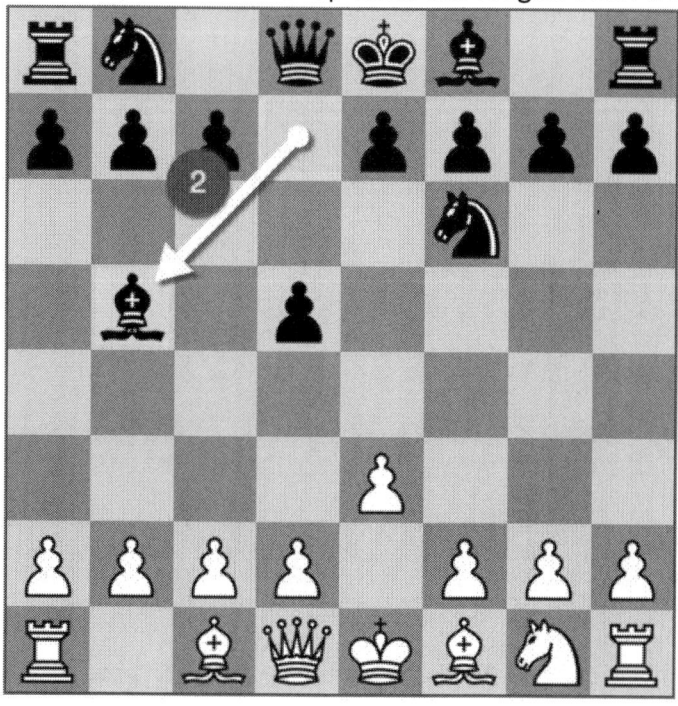

In the **third move** we take Black's Bishop. See the **image below**. Now, both sides lost a piece, I'm not necessarily recommending you make this move. But, the point is to see far enough ahead to know that if Black capture our Knight, we can capture back.

BUT we would have needed to visualize the result in our head **three moves in advance** BEFORE we moved the Knight. It's seeing three moves in advance that is the purpose of this exercise.

In this example, the exchange is even. We lose a Knight and Black loses a Bishop. But, in many cases, seeing three moves in advance can win you pieces. The reverse is also true; if you fail to see moves in advance, you can lose pieces.

85

Now that you've seen what it looks like, there are basically three parts to seeing moves in advance.
1. **Visualize** the move you want to make
2. **Predict** the move your opponent will make
3. Visualize your **reaction** to your opponent's move

An easier way to remember it is **Visualize, Predict, React**. Then, remember the final image.

EXERCISE #1

Now that you understand seeing moves in advance. Let's practice. In the **image below**, you would like to move the White Knight to the square indicated by the arrow. Visualize three moves ahead. Count one, two, and three on each move. And then remember what the **final image** looks like at the end of the third move. Here's a hint: White ends up a piece ahead.

Visualize three moves ahead.
*Use **Visualize, Predict, React,** or*
Count: One, two, three out loud for each move.
Remember what the final image looks like.

Did you do it? Let's walk through how this three move exchange should happen.

We **Visualize** the Knight moving to our desired square.

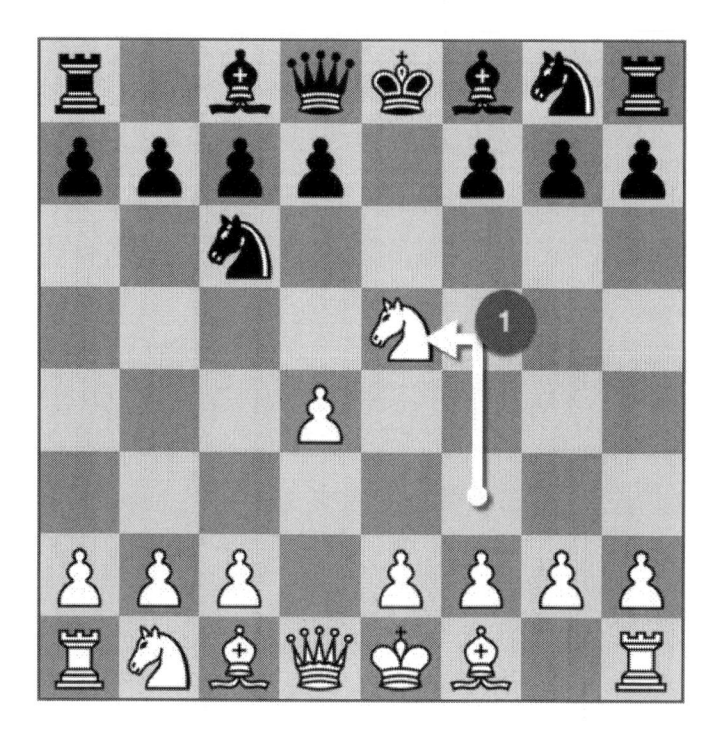

We **Predict** the Knight will attack back.

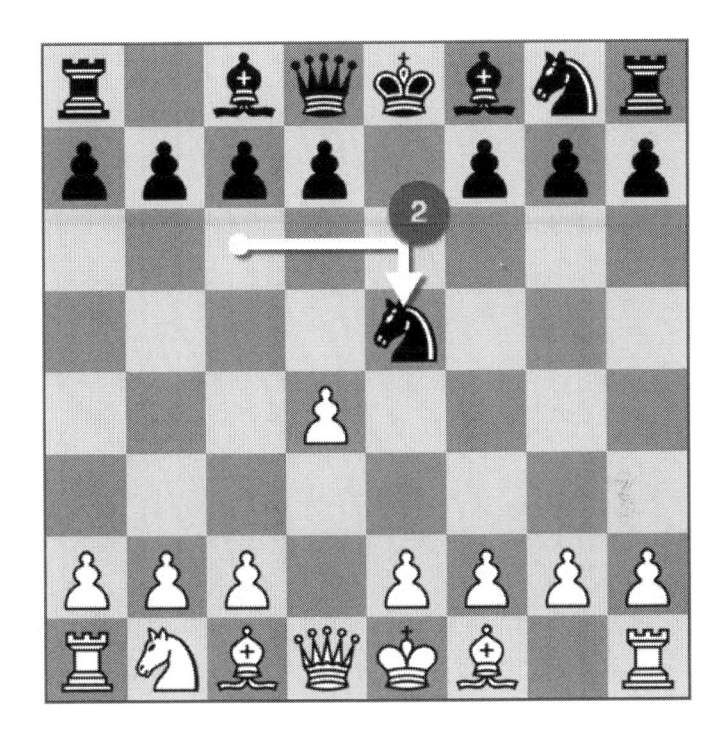

We **React** by attacking the Knight, and we end up a Pawn ahead.

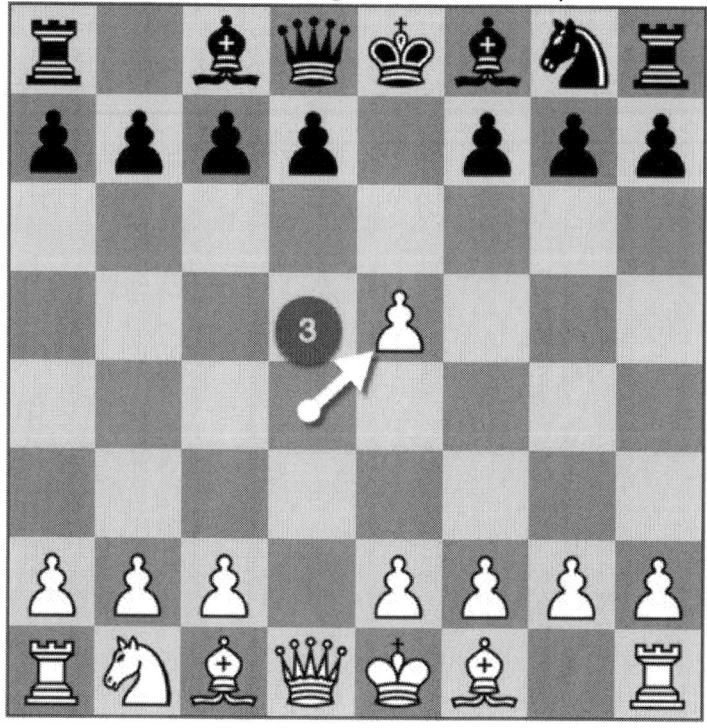

If you visualized a different sequence for this exchange, that's okay! The point is predicting three moves in advance by visualizing what will happen.

If you found this exercise difficult that's because it is! But the more you play, the more you become used to it. Let's try one more time.

EXERCISE #2

In the **image below**, you're playing White. You would like to move the White Rook to the square indicated by the arrow and an exchange is likely to take place. Visualize three moves ahead. Count one, two, and three on each move. And then remember what the image looks like at the end of the third move.

Visualize three moves ahead.
Use Visualize, Predict, React, *or*
Count: One, two, three out loud for each move.
Remember what the final image looks like.

We **Visualize** our Rook moving to block our King.

If the Black Rook moves out of the way, he'll lose his last Pawn, so we **Predict** Black will capture our Rook.

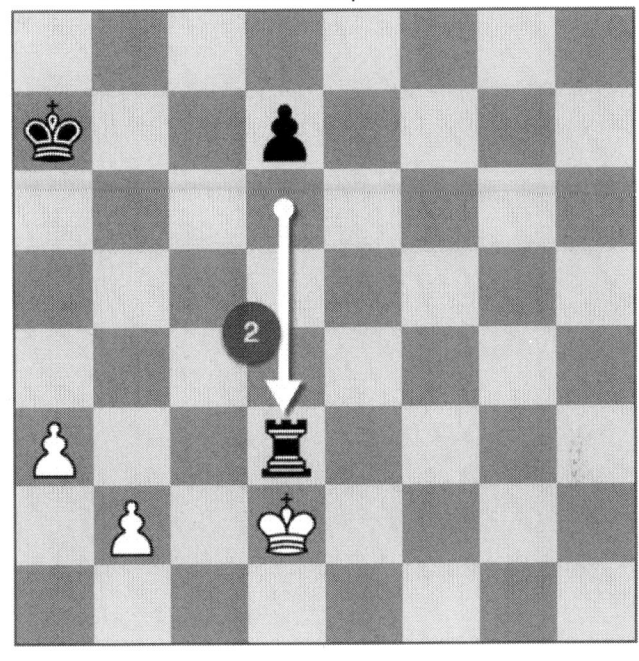

We **React** in the best possible way, by taking the Black Rook.

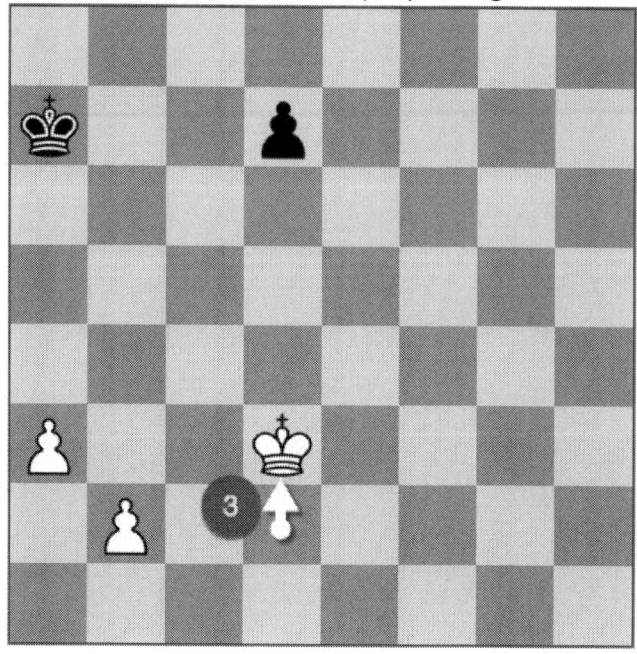

Again, if you didn't get the exercise the way I got them, that's okay! As long as you saw three moves in your mind's eye you're good.

The point isn't to test if you're right or wrong, it's to exercise your brain and get it used to thinking ahead. The more you play Chess the more you will naturally think more and more moves ahead. Chess masters are known for thinking 10 or more moves ahead! But for now, to stay a step ahead of your opponent, **think three moves ahead.**

VISUAL GAME SUMMARY

To summarize the visual game for beginners.

In order to keep your pieces safe and plan effective attacks, you'll need to **Visualize** the movement and attack path of the active pieces on the board. An **Active Piece** is any piece that can affect the game within one to two moves.

It's not enough to Visualize and think ahead on your own strategy, you must also **Predict your Opponent's Intentions**. This is how you keep your pieces safe, and launch effective attacks.

Every time you move a piece, before you let go of the piece, run through your **Mental Checklist**. Check to make sure no enemy pieces can capture it and you don't leave any other pieces vulnerable by moving it.

Chess isn't as easy as seeing the moves on the board, in order to win at the beginner level you'll need to **Think Three Moves Ahead**. As you become more accustomed to the game, you'll be able to think more and more moves in advance.

CONCLUSION

Now you know the fundamentals of Chess. You know how to play and with practice you'll know how to win. But you're probably wondering, "where do I go from here?"

First, go out and play a game. If you can, bust out your Chess board and play against someone close to the same level as you. If you don't have a board or there's no one available, Chess.com's live Chess is an incredible resource for playing Chess. You can play people across the world and easily find people around the same level as you.

I also recommend the Chess with Friends app for Android and iphone. This app lets you search through your contacts or Facebook friends for people to play Chess against.

When you want to continue sharpening and honing your Chess skills, I recommend you get the sequel: Chess: Conquer your Friends with 8 Easy Principles. These are the 8 highest impact Chess principles you can use against your friends. It's everything from how to play the opening to how to recognize easy checkmates in one move.

Now, you might have an undeniable edge against your beginner friends, but hey, there's no reason you can't share these secrets. Now is your chance to take what you've learned and give back to the community. Show a younger sibling your techniques, encourage learning and progress, or teach a friend how to play the game of wits, war, and intellect, or...

Keep your secret Chess abilities to yourself.

I won't tell...I promise.

DOWNLOAD YOUR FREE EBOOK!

Top 6 MOVES TO AVOID in the Opening

CHESS

A Cheat Sheet for Casual Players and Post-Beginners

MAXEN TARAFA

Your first 5 to 10 moves are the most critical moves in the entire game. In this **FREE mini-ebook**, I show you **6 moves NOT to make** in the Opening. By simply NOT making these moves you gain a huge edge on your opponents. Join the casual Chess revolution today! Enter your email to download and receive free book offers and updates! 20 pages.

Download here

TAKE YOUR SKILLS TO THE NEXT LEVEL!

Now available in paperback!

CONQUER YOUR FRIENDS with 8 Easy Principles

CHESS

A Cheat Sheet for Casual Players and Post-Beginners

MAXEN TARAFA

If you liked this book, you'll enjoy the next installment. Chess mastery takes years, but to beat your friends? All you need is 8 easy principles. No history. No notation. Improve your Chess game today!

Buy eBook or Paperback from Amazon

Bonus Material

FAQ

Beginners have lots of questions. And one book simply isn't enough to cover them all.

That's why I created a bonus section in the new edition of this book.

Most questions beginners have aren't just about the game itself, but about things like etiquette, where to play, and what kind of board to play on. The following is a compilation of the top Chess questions from beginners I've received and answers to them!

This is bonus material made for you in the new edition, so if you like the book and the new material, the only favor I ask is that you…

★★★★★
Leave an Excellent Review!

To leave a review, go here.
(Or, just click past the end of the book in your Kindle)

Boards, Pieces, and Equipment

What is a novelty board? Why don't you like novelty boards?

A novelty board is any board that features unusual piece or board design, such as Simpsons characters or Super Mario characters.

While these chessboards are cool, I would only recommend them when you're advanced in Chess and have truly internalized the pieces and their functions. I don't recommend them for beginners because sometimes it can be hard to tell which piece is which with novelty boards.

Personally, I try to avoid novelty boards or any board that even slightly distracts me from the game. If I have to think about my move even a fraction of a second longer because I'm using a novelty board, I'm not pleased.

Basically, I would rather win than play on a cool board. But, to each their own.

Are there other versions of Chess?

Yes, literally hundreds. There are other versions of playing chess with roughly the same board and with modified boards.

For example, I've enjoyed four person chess where every player has a set of pieces and all players play on the same board.

I've also enjoyed playing Crazyhouse Chess with my students. The basic gameplay goes like this: whenever you capture a piece, you get to keep that piece (in your own color) and place it anywhere on the board.

For a list of the hundreds of variations of chess, you can search "List of Chess variants" on Wikipedia and it will show you how to play many of them.

But for the most part, I'm a purist. Regular chess is the most universal game and I'm always striving to get better at it. I recommend beginners play regular Chess for a few months until they've internalized the basics before playing any other variants.

What kind of Chessboard should I buy?

If you're playing at home, I would recommend a wooden chess board around 10" x 10".

If you think you may be traveling with the chessboard or playing in the car, I would recommend getting a magnetic chessboard. This magnetizes the pieces to the board so they don't all fall off if you tip the board.

You may also want to think about storage. Some chessboards have a compartment inside to store pieces. One of the biggest blockers of regular chess play for beginners is not having all your pieces, so a built-in compartment can be helpful.

Here's a chessboard on Amazon I recommend that meets all the criteria I just mentioned: Wooden Chessboard

If you're a Chess student, you may want to get a vinyl board with a carrying case. These are the easiest to roll up and transport if you're moving from class to class. They also have the coordinates written on the sides in case you need to record your games.

Here's a good one on Amazon: Vinyl Chessboard

(By the way, I don't receive a commission or anything. I just like to recommend specifics.)

As mentioned earlier, I do not recommend getting a novelty board or any "pretty" or "cool" boards as these can distract from the game. I also try to avoid glass chessboards when possible.

Do I need a Chess clock?

A chess clock can be useful if you want to play faster, keep you and your opponent on your toes, or if you're serious about playing tournaments.

Chess clocks cost anywhere from $15 to $70. Quality does make a difference here as the cheapest end of chess clocks will easily break.

Here's a good simple, digital chess clock that I've used with students that's only $18: Digital Chess Clock

There are also tons of free chess clock apps if you have a smartphone handy. I typically use an app when I'm playing my friends because I usually don't have a chess clock on hand.

My favorite is called **Chess Clock by Chess.com.** You can find it in just about any app store.

How do I play with a clock?

The basic idea is that you and your opponent each get a set amount of time on your side of the clock.

For example, you each get 10 minutes on uour clock.

While you are making your move or deciding your move, your clock is running. If your ten minutes runs out, you lose – even if you have all your pieces left. So, you want to play as fast as possible to conserve your time.

Also, you are supposed to hit your clock with the same hand you use to move the piece. Once you hit your clock, the time starts going down for your opponent.

Playing with a Chess is clock is fun and it can help you become faster and better at Chess.

Can I play if I have pieces, but no Chessboard?

You can make one! Just find a picture of a chessboard online and re-create it.

Use a ruler, if possible. And remember, there's 64 squares or 8x8 squares. And white on the right!

If you have a checkers board, you can also use that.

What if my Chess set is missing a piece?

Uggh, the dreaded missing piece! Obviously, the best defense against missing pieces is to not lose them in the first place. That's why I recommend buying a chessboard with a built-in Chess compartment if you think you might need one. It also helps when there are slots for each specific piece so you can tell if a piece is missing.

Otherwise, you can also write or draw the piece on a piece of paper. Or, replace it with a piece from another board game and just agree with your opponent on which piece it is. But the more of these makeshift pieces you have, the harder it gets to remember which is which.

If your piece is permanently missing, I would highly recommend buying a new set of pieces as this can affect play quality and could inhibit your growth as a chess player.

What is Chess notation? Why don't you use it?

Chess notation or algebraic notation is a system for writing the location and actions of pieces on a Chessboard. Even though many "experts" and "academics" don't like my approach, I don't typically use notation in my books because I find it's too abstract for people who simply want to play among friends. But if you're interested in playing in a club or a tournament it's good to know.

For example, in the following image, you'll notice the numbers **1 through 8** written along the side and the letters **A through H** written below.

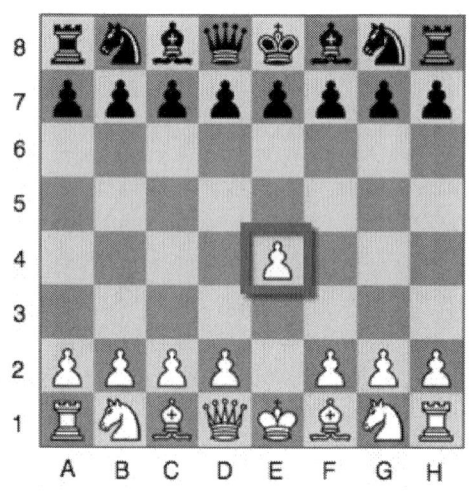

You can use these coordinates to locate the exact square on a board.

The letters identify **Files**, which are columns on the board. The numbers identify **Ranks**, which are the rows.

For example, if I wanted to talk about the highlighted Pawn, I would first identify the File it's on. So I find the column the Pawn is on and below is the letter 'E'. The Pawn is on the E file.

Then I find the row the Pawn is on. According to my coordinates, this Pawn is on the 4th row. So, the 4th rank.

To put it together, I would call this the e4 Pawn.

There is a lot more to notation language and another resource can explain it in more detail. Many Chess books write entire games and provide most of their instruction using notation, so it's useful to know.

But you won't need to know it for my books.

Gameplay

Why do I have to take a turn? Can I skip my turn?

Haha. No, you can't skip your turn, even if you volunteer. It's simply one of the rules of Chess. Be prepared for your turn and make your move when it comes!

Why can't Pawns move backwards?

Good question. It's simply one of the rules of Chess. Also, it would be a really long, boring game if 8 Pawns were able to move backwards. Plus, it's way better to promote your Pawn to a Queen or any other piece when it reaches the end.

Can I keep playing after I'm checkmated?

Nope, sorry! The game ends when you or your opponent is checkmated. But this is good news because now you can start a new game and learn something new.

Can the King ever move more than one space?

The only time the King moves more than one space is during Castling.

Can my pieces move off the board and onto a square on the other side of the board?

Haha. No. The edge of the board is a finite barrier. Think of the edges as walls.

Can I castle if I've moved my King?

Nope.

Can I castle if I've moved my Rook?

If it's the rook you're planning to Castle with, then no. If you've moved the other Rook that you're not castling with then it's okay.

How many times can I castle per game?

Once.

Can I have more than one Queen? Or, more than two Rooks, Knights, or Bishops?

Yes, this is possible only through promotion. When you move your Pawn to the opposite end of the board you can promote it to any piece you want except for a Pawn or a King.

That means you could theoretically have 9 Queens, 10 Rooks, or 10 Knights, or 10 Bishops (but it's extremely unlikely your opponent will let you have that many). For beginners, it's almost always best to promote your Pawn to a Queen.

Is there any way to get a piece back once I've lost it?

There's only one way to get a piece back that you've lost and that's if you promote your Pawn.

And technically, you're converting a Pawn into a new piece rather than getting it back. But, if you'd like to think about it as "getting it back," you can.

My Pawn is stuck, can he move sideways/backwards/jump other pieces?

Nope! Pawns can only move forward, forward-diagonally (when capturing) or promote when they reach the opposite end of the board.

You could also capture the piece blocking your Pawn so that it's no longer in the way.

Do I have to move the Pawn two spaces on the first move?

Nope. In fact, it may be beneficial to only move it one space.

If my opponent doesn't move out of check, can I take the King and win the game?

Nice try! But no. You'll just have to remind your opponent that they're in Check and wait for them to move it to a legal square.

The only other thing remotely close is En Passant, which is explained in special moves section of *How to Play Chess for (Absolute) Beginners.*

Can I jump over another piece with a Queen, Bishop, Rook, or Pawn?

Nope. Only the Knight can jump other pieces.

If two pieces attack each other, do I have to take it?

Nope. You can also just move out of the way. Or, you can let your opponent capture it if you'd like, but I wouldn't let your opponent capture your piece unless it's part of a bigger strategy.

Can I capture my own piece?
No.

Can a Pawn capture a piece of higher value?

Yes, a Pawn can capture any piece as long as it's a legal move. So, it can't capture a King, but it *can* capture a Queen, Rook, Knight, or Bishop.

Can I move a piece onto a square that is already occupied by one of my own pieces?

Move two pieces onto the same square? No, you can't do that in Chess.

Can I capture two pieces at the same time?

Nope, one piece at a time.

Can I capture pieces with my King?

Yes, the King can capture any piece as long as it's a legal move. For example, the King can't capture a piece if it's being protected by another opposing piece.

Can Black move first?

Nope. White must move first.

My King and my opponent's King are the only pieces left? How do I win?

Actually, that is a draw by insufficient material. You both tie. You'll want to end the game and start again. You simply can't win when there are only two Kings left.

What's the fastest way to win? Is a 2-move checkmate possible?

There is a 2-move checkmate, but your opponent would have to make a really bad move in the beginning. The 4-move checkmate is much more common and I actually explain how to do that in my book *Chess: Conquer Your Friends with 4 Daredevil Openings*.

Can I castle if I've already been in check?

If you are currently in check, you can't castle. If you *were* in check and now you're out of check, you can still castle as long as you follow all the other castling rules.

Can I castle the long way toward the Rook on the Queenside?

Yes, you can. Just remember your King always moves two spaces towards the Rook and then the Rook moves to the other side of the King.

Can a game end in a draw?

Yes, it can. I don't go into it much in this book since draws can be really confusing to beginners. But, there are a few ways a game can end in a draw.

Here are a few ways:
- Stalemate
- Three-Move Repetition
- 50 Move Rule
- Insufficient Material
- Draw by Agreement

A **Stalemate** is when your King is not in check and you have no other legal moves.

Three-Move Repetition is when you repeat the exact same position three times.

50-Move Rule is when you and your opponent make fifty moves without capturing a piece. This results in a draw.

Insufficient Material is when you don't have enough pieces to checkmate your opponent. For example, when you and your opponent only have a King and a King left on the board, it's a draw. You can't checkmate with only a King.

You also can't checkmate with:
- A King and Bishop vs. a King
- A King and Knight vs. a King
- A King and Bishop vs. a King and Bishop (when Bishops are on opposite-colored squares)

Draw by Agreement is when two players agree to a draw for any reason.

A Draw means no one wins or loses. Both players tie. And in tournaments a draw usually results in both players gaining 0.5 points, (which is not nearly as good as winning).

For the most part, beginners should focus on winning the game. I see too many beginners get to the end of the game and not know how to checkmate and agree to draw with their opponent.

I recommend beginners avoid draws by agreement at all costs and learn how to checkmate, as that is the essence of the game.

If you want to learn more advanced strategy about how to use draws or stalemates strategically in your play, I suggest you check out the next book in this series: *Chess: Conquer Your Friends with 8 Easy Principles.*

What is a legal/illegal move?

A **legal** move is any move that is allowed by the rules of the game.

An **illegal** move would be a move that is not allowed by the rules of the game.

Will you be arrested if you make an illegal move in Chess? No. But, if you're in a tournament an illegal move can be bad.

In casual play, if you make an illegal move your opponent will probably just ask you to re-make the move.

Etiquette

What do I do if the board and all the pieces get knocked over?

If you and your opponent can remember *exactly* where the pieces went, you can set up the board as it was.

If not, I'd suggest you just set up the board from the beginning and start a new game!

What do I do if I realize I was in check three moves later?

If you realize after the fact that you *were* in check and you didn't remove yourself from check as you're obligated, you and your opponent should take those three moves back IF you can remember them. If you can't, then you might as well just play from where you are.

If I play White the first game, do I keep playing White the second game or do we switch?

You ought to switch sides with your opponent every game you play. This ensures that you're both learning both Black and White gameplay.

But if both you and your opponent are okay with playing the same color, there's no official rules on that in casual play.

Does it really matter who plays White or Black pieces? Aren't they the same?

The two sides are not *exactly* the same. Because White always plays first White is always a more offensive position to play. White Openings tend to take advantage of the fact that White sets the pace.

Black openings tend to be more defensive or responsive to White's first moves.

Also, the board is set up slightly differently on each side. For example, the Black Queen starts to the right of the Black King. If you tried to play a White opening with this set up, it would be a different game.

How do you decide who plays White?

The best way I've found to do this is to take a Black and White piece and hide them behind my back from my opponent. One piece in my right hand the other in my left. I then ask my opponent to choose an arm.

If he selects my right arm, then show him the piece in that hand. If it's a White piece, he plays white. If it's a Black piece, he plays black.

If that doesn't work, you can also flip a coin.

How long should a Chess game take?

Some games take hours or even years. Some take less than 10 minutes.

My games with friends when we're not using a clock will usually last about 20 minutes.

If you're an absolute beginner and want to use a clock, I would recommend starting with 20 minutes on your clock and 20 minutes on your opponent's clock. I would soon graduate to 10 minutes on each clock. The more games you play, the better you'll get. In general, I would learn how to play faster.

If you run out of time with a clock, can you count the value of the pieces?

This is typically not how it works. The piece values are meant to be relative values not absolute values.

Usually, the player whose time runs out first loses.

What happens if I move a Pawn to my opponent's end of the board?

If you move your Pawn to the opposite end of the board, you can promote that Pawn to any piece you want except for a Pawn or King. I discuss this further in the Special Moves section of How to Play Chess for (Absolute) Beginners.

If I move another piece (other than a Pawn) to my opponent's end of the board, can I promote it?

Nope. Only Pawns.

Can I take back a move I've made? If I touch a piece, do I have to move it?

In casual play, you and your opponent may agree to a take-back rule.

In tournaments or serious play, if you touch a piece you must move it and you absolutely cannot take moves back – unless there are unusual circumstances.

I recommend getting into the habit, even in casual play, to not take moves back.

Can I move one of my opponent's pieces if they get up to go the bathroom?

Haha. Good try! But no.

How do I become fast? How do I convince my opponent to move faster?

To become fast at chess, you'll want to start playing with a clock. Start playing with 20 minutes on your clock. Then, you can push yourself to play with 10 minutes on your clock. Then, you can try five!

If your opponent is a slow player, you may want to convince them to agree to use a chess clock with you.

Can I have a friend or partner who helps me make moves or moves for me?

This is frowned upon. Chess is a game between two minds. Observers should not recommend or even hint that they "know a great move."

In a tournament, a talking participant would be removed from the play area. In casual play, it's not so serious, but the best etiquette is for observers to keep speaking to a minimum and definitely not suggest or hint at moves.

What do I do if I need to stop a game and resume later?

If your board is in a safe place, you can leave it exactly as it is and come back to it later.

If it might get bumped or the pieces moved around, you might want to take a picture with your phone.

What if my opponent cheats?

In casual play, there's not much you can do. Just don't play with them again if they do it consistently.

If it's a dispute about the rules, you can usually look up rule specifics on Google, Wikipedia, or even this book.

If I promote my Pawn and I don't have extra pieces, how do I use that piece?

Many boards come with an extra Queen. So, if you're promoting to a Queen use that.

If your board doesn't have an extra Queen and any of the Rooks have been captured, you can try turning your Rook upside down on the board and agreeing with your opponent that it is now your second Queen.

When I take a piece from the board, where does it go?

I would place it on the side of the board or closest to me off the side of the board. I like to place all my captured pieces in the same area, so I can keep track of which pieces have been removed and who is "winning." I also like to place them in order of height or value, which helps me keep track of how much me or my opponent has lost.

When should I resign? I should never give up, right?

There are different philosophies on this. If I was playing a serious game, I would probably continue no matter how grim my outlook is.

I would recommend pushing through for most beginners because no matter how bad it looks, there is a chance your opponent might cause a draw or stalemate you. Then you tie and don't lose.

If I'm planning to play several games with friends; and, I'm losing big time; and, I believe there's a very slim chance I will win or my opponent will stalemate me, I will sometimes resign so that me and my friend can play a new game – especially if the time we have together is short.

Otherwise, I fight til the bitter end!

My King can't legally move anywhere and he's not in check. Is it stalemate?

If your King is the last piece left, yes that would be stalemate. If you still have pieces left and they can move, then it's not stalemate yet.

Chess Venues, Chess Players, and Chess Resources

Who is the most famous Chess player? Who are some famous Chess players?

The most famous Chess player in the US is probably Bobby Fischer. Currently, one of the most famous is Magnus Carlsen. Other famous Chess players include Boris Spassky, Garry Kasparov, Anatoly Karpov, Jose Raul Capablanca, Judit Polgar, and Paul Morphy to name a few.

What is a rating?

A rating is a system for estimating your relative skill to other players. When you play in tournaments or online you often receive a rating.

You gain or lose points based on who you beat.

Most absolute beginners start with a rating of about 100-600. But, ratings can go as high as 2000 and beyond. For example, the top rated Chess player in the world, Magnus Carlsen has a rating of 2882 as of May 2014.

In casual play, your rating is not affected.

Can I play Chess on the internet?

Yes, my favorite website is Chess.com.

Can I play against my computer?

Yes, many computers have chess games on them. However, I don't like to play against computers because they don't make natural moves. It's usually best to play against a human.

What is the difference between playing at home and playing at a club or tournament?

Rules are much more strict in a tournament. For example, you can't speak or check your phone. You'll typically use a clock.

Can you play Chess professionally?

Yes, some exceptional chess players become professionals. They are often sponsored the same way a pro basketball or football player is sponsored and may receive money from winning tournaments.

How do you become a professional Chess player?

Good question. You can become a professional by getting really good at playing chess. You'll probably want to undergo serious formal training with a coach or mentor.

Can I talk or distract my opponent while he's playing?

In casual play, it could be considered rude to talk excessively. At the same time, a little chatting is typically expected.

If you're playing a serious game or tournament game, talking can get you removed from the match.

If your opponent asks you not to talk, it's polite not to talk.

If you're a chess student, you should get used to not talking during games.

Chess Myths

Is Chess for geniuses? Can only geniuses play Chess? Do I have to be smart to be good at Chess?

Chess is an intellectual game. But, smart or genius is a relative term. Plenty of "regular" people play chess. I don't claim to be a genius whatsoever. Don't get me wrong, it takes practice, study, and work to get good, but anyone can do it with the right attitude and resources (starting with this book).

Why is Chess so hard? I want to go back to Checkers.

Yes, Chess has a lot more variables and complexities than checkers. But once you understand Chess, you'll probably never go back to Checkers. You can play Chess for 80 years and never know everything in the game. You're always learning something new.

I'm not an analytical/calculating/numbers type person. Can I be good at Chess?

I was an English major. I never thought I'd have the "right mind" for Chess. But, with a lot of work, I got quite good at it and now I know few people who can beat me.

I have bad luck. Can I be good at Chess?

The beautiful thing about Chess is that luck is only a very small factor. Some Chess players calculate outcomes 30 moves in advance. If you learn how to play well and right, you won't win or lose because of luck, it's because either you did or didn't see a move coming in advance. And that's a skill that can be learned.

Do I have to memorize patterns to be good at Chess?

A lot of people are intimidated by having to "memorize patterns" in Chess. What they're probably thinking of are tactics, checkmate patterns, and openings.

I explain all of these things in the simplest possible way (with pictures) in the rest of my Chess books. If you start with my books, you can probably go on to learn just about any pattern and it won't seem so intimidating.

If someone beats me in Chess, are they smarter than me?

Contrary to popular opinion, Chess is not an intelligence contest. Your skill in Chess is a measurement only in your skill in Chess. That's it.

Winning or losing does not mean you're smarter or less smart. It just means the circumstances and decisions you and your opponent made in that game led to you winning or losing.

With practice and training, *anyone* can get better at Chess.

Isn't Chess a kids' game?

Hahahaha. This question makes me laugh. Yes, it's a board game. But there are so many strategies, tactics, and life lessons to learn from Chess...not even one lifetime can contain them all.

Calling Chess a kid's game would be like calling Basketball a kid's game. Did Bobby Fisher put any less work into his craft than Michael Jordan or Kobe Bryant? It's hard to measure, but I'm positive he did!

For the right player, Chess is a sport and is an entire career for some people.

Not to mention, there are many critical lifelong lessons that can be learned from playing Chess, including: patience, strategy, self-improvement, sportsmanship, mental athleticism, and camaraderie.

I can honestly say Chess is one of the most important things I've ever learned and anyone who improves their Chess game will also benefit in many more areas of their life than simply Chess.

Hey Reader,
You made it to the end.
I hope you learned something new and cool.

If you liked the book, do me a favor and...

*****
Leave an Excellent Review!

Good reviews help indie authors like me write more books for readers like you. (Plus, I sometimes send free books to reviewers who write great reviews.)

To leave a review, go here.
(Or, just click to the next page in your Kindle)

CONQUER YOUR FRIENDS WITH 8 EASY PRINCIPLES

Table of Contents

The Beginner Challenge

The Board and the Players

The Knight

Visualizing Active Pieces
    Exercise #1
    Exercise #2

Take your skills to the next level!
    Chapter 1: Improve your Chess Game Faster…the Skill Artist Way
    Chapter 2: How to Learn From this Book
    Chapter 3: 8 Principles to Conquer your friends
        Principle #1: Control The Center
        Principle #2: Trade All the way down
        Principle #3: The Weapons of Chess
        Principle #4: Castle Early, Castle Often
        Principle #5: Keep your Queen Back
        Principle #6: Win the Queen Race
        Principle #7: Fight for a Stalemate
        Principle #8: Watch for the Weak Back Rank
        8 Principles Closing
    Chapter 4: Tips to Accelerate Your Learning
    Conclusion
    Resources

DOWNLOAD YOUR FREE EBOOK!

Top 6 MOVES TO AVOID in the Opening

CHESS

A Cheat Sheet for Casual Players and Post-Beginners

MAXEN TARAFA

Your first 5 to 10 moves are the most critical moves in the entire game. In this **FREE ebook**, I show you **6 moves NOT to make** in the Opening. By simply NOT making these moves you gain a huge edge on your opponents. Join the casual Chess revolution today! Enter your email to download and receive free book offers and updates! 20 pages.

Scroll to the end of the book for your free download.

Chess: Conquer your Friends with 8 Easy Principles

Copyright © 2015 by Maxen Tarafa

All rights reserved. This book or any portion thereof
may not be reproduced or used in any manner whatsoever without the
express written permission of the publisher except for the use of brief
quotations in a book review.
www.theskillartistsguide.com

CHAPTER 1: IMPROVE YOUR CHESS GAME FASTER...THE SKILL ARTIST WAY

My name is Maxen R. Tarafa, and I'm a Skill Artist. No, I'm not going to ask you to find a walnut under a cup or join a pyramid scheme. I want to show you how you can play Chess at an intermediate level in an alarmingly short amount of time.

If you're anything like me, you want to play a good or *very good* game of Chess, but you're not interested in becoming the next Garry Kasparov. You just want to know a few moves and maybe **conquer all your friends!** Enter the art of learning new skills. Or, what I call Skill Art.

My approach is simple. In most any skill, if you learn and apply five to ten of the most critical lessons, you'll be at least twice as good as the beginner. However, most books written by experts are either going to be an A to Z instruction book or they're going to be designed for the in-crowd.

Let me be the first to say, I'm not an expert in Chess. I'm a guy who learns skills in a short amount of time, and I want to give you an extended cheat sheet to help you do what I did, but faster.

I guarantee there's going to be a lot of "Chess experts" who don't like this. I'm ready for the hate mail. After all, Chess is supposed to be hard and complicated and cold and logical and emotionless, right? But I'm confident that if you read this book and practice the 8 principles I provide, not only will you have a great time reading it, you will also have a significant edge over your opponents.

How am I so confident they'll work? First, they worked for me. In college, my roommate and I played Chess regularly. Neither of us was trained, but we enjoyed playing. After I graduated from college, I wanted to get better and I dedicated myself to playing Chess for at least 3 hours a day for about 3 months. When I started out my rating was in the low 600s.

I'd been playing Chess for more than 10 years and I was only in the 600s! (Just a point of reference, master level is 2200 and up). After studying everything I could find on the internet and practicing, I more than doubled my rating up to 1300! These eight principles stand out to me as the most important.

Second, I taught these principles to people I know. When my brother was 9 years old, the only thing he knew was how to move the pieces. I taught him these 8 principles and a week later he was beating 16 and 17 year olds.

There is one principle in particular that I taught to an exceptionally talented student named Eduardo when I was a Chess coach at my friend's high school. He applied one principle and it *changed his game completely*. None of us could beat him after that—including me!

When I was preparing to write this book, I told my friend Gus, who trained competitively as a kid, that I was writing a guide for beginners about eight principles that will greatly impact their game. He said, "Oh yeah, you can totally tell a difference between trained players and people who have never studied Chess." He then went on to list four of the eight techniques I was already planning to use!

Before I started practicing Chess, I thought only "logical" people could be good at Chess. As a writing and arts oriented person, I never thought

I could be competitive with my more "logical" friends. What I realized after training myself is no matter who you are you can learn ANYTHING. If you can read, practice, and use a computer you can learn these techniques in a week!

I won't mention any names. But some of my longtime friends and family who used to destroy me when I was young can't beat me anymore. One of my friends actually said to me, "Dude, I haven't beaten you since you started playing on the Internet." What I didn't tell him was that I wasn't just playing. I was training.

All in all, these are some of the nastiest and most effective techniques for post-beginners and they are sure to help you conquer your friends. Just remember, with great power comes great responsibility.

Sincerely,

Maxen R. Tarafa

www.theskillartistsguide.com

CHAPTER 2: HOW TO LEARN FROM THIS BOOK

Unlike most Chess books, in this book you'll find no complex Chess notation. You also won't find lengthy discussions of the games of Chess Masters. There are only principles, simple (if crude) illustrations of those principles, and links to videos or external website to help you understand the principle.

I'm assuming a few things in the title of this book. First, I'm assuming your friends aren't formally trained Chess players. If they are, and you want to beat them, this book can give you a big leg up. Second, I'm assuming you already know the basics of Chess. I created this book for casual Chess players who have played for years but never studied the game. If you're an absolute beginner you can still use this book, but you might want to review the basics.

Chess Basics

I've recently created a book for absolute beginners. It's called How to Play Chess: For (Absolute) Beginners: The Journey to your Empire Begins Here. If you're looking for the basics, it is the prequel to this book, and it shows you how to remember and apply the basics from how to move the pieces to how to checkmate. In my (humble) opinion, this is the best book out there for beginners. Click here to buy your copy.

Measure your Progress

When creating this book, I designed each chapter to be as short and easy to remember as possible. Of course, there's more to learn, but that will come later. The important thing is that you learn and remember the principle and then practice.

I would suggest that before you start learning the 8 principles that you go to Chess.com (You'll see a lot references to Chess.com. I swear they're not a sponsor, I just really like the website). Sign up for a free account and play Live Chess. Live Chess is cool because you can play people from across the world and even chat with them if you'd like. But the point is to get yourself a rating.

I know you mainly just want to stomp on *your* friends via Chess. But the reason I say to get a rating is that you can easily accelerate your learning when you can set measurable goals and work to obtain them. If you never know where you're starting, you'll never know how far you've come, or how far you *want* to go.

Links and Videos

A note on the links and videos, I use a lot of them. If your device is connected to the Internet, you can just click on the link and a browser window should open. If it's not connected to the Internet, I provided the title of the video so you can easily just search it in Youtube with your computer.

You don't have to watch every single video, but if you want to get a better idea of the principle, check it out. I realize Youtube videos probably aren't the most academically sound way to teach. But luckily, I don't care! As a skill artist, I look for clear, quality information, and if it can help me learn quickly, I use it!

Engage your Senses

As you read, you may want to play with a Chessboard next to you. Or with a Chess Program (such as Chess.com) open in a separate window. It will help to practice the principles as you go (especially if you're a kinesthetic learner).

The principles are listed in order of what you are most likely to encounter. After you've read the book, and you're ready to practice, re-read the principles you want to practice. Then, apply them, keeping them in mind as you play.

Alright, let's get to the good stuff. Here are 8 principles that will help you conquer your friends in Chess.

CHAPTER 3: 8 PRINCIPLES TO CONQUER YOUR FRIENDS

PRINCIPLE #1: CONTROL THE CENTER

You know how I can tell a Chess Player from a Monopoly player? It's their first move. Most novices choose a piece they think is interesting. Some choose a piece they think is safe. Both are fine as long as you do one thing...**Control the Center.** Whoever controls the center controls the game.

What do I mean by the center? **In the picture below**, I've highlighted the four squares that make up the center. Think of these as your **Power Squares.**

In the beginning of the game, every move you make should fight to control those four squares. That means most likely your first move will be one of those center Pawns followed by your Knights and your Bishops. **In the picture below,** I show what your pieces would look like if they were developed to control those four squares.

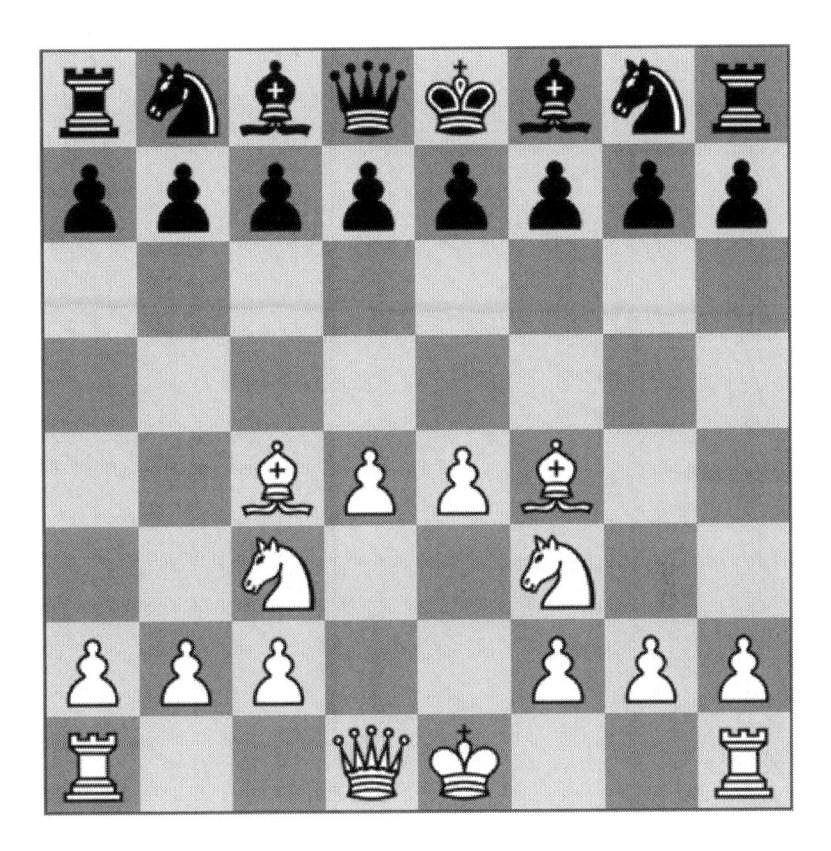

Notice that each of the middle squares is poised for attack by at least one (sometimes two) of white's pieces. This development shows the best control of the center. Of course, this arrangement is nearly impossible in a real game. But when you're choosing an opening or creating an opening for yourself, keep in mind that any decent opening will use a variation of this set-up.

Why is it so important to control the center?

Let me put it this way. Controlling the Center is like controlling the stereo when you're with your jerkhole older brother on a road trip. If you connect *your* iPhone first, you can choose from a variety of your favorite musicians. If your jerkhole older brother connects his, you can only choose among Justin Bieber, Nickelback, and Chumbawumba and you're going to have to choose among *his* favorite bands. Which would you rather have?

Center control is closely related to development. If you control the center, it makes it very hard for your opponent to develop his pieces (or bad taste in music) past the center or move his good pieces toward your King. The center is the fastest and easiest place to damage your opponent from. So, the person who controls it has far more opportunities to attack.

What this means is: You want to move your central Pawns, Knights, and Bishops first. You want to move your Rooks and the six side Pawns last.

Controlling the center requires a good opening. There are literally hundreds of openings to choose from, but I guarantee they all try to **Control the Center.**

Update: I recently released a new Chess book on Amazon about Openings. If you want to learn more ways to control the center or how to make your first 5 moves. Click here.

PRINCIPLE #2: TRADE ALL THE WAY DOWN

This one's a two-parter that will increase your offensive power tenfold.

Part 1: **Know the Piece Values.** Many beginning players don't know exactly what each piece is worth. Most people know that Pawns are the least valuable, but you need to know the exact point value of each piece in a pinch. Here's a breakdown:

Piece	Image	Value	Explanation
King	♚	Ultimate	The **King** is infinitely valuable. If you checkmate the King, the game's over.
Queen	♛	9 pts.	The **Queen** is the most powerful piece on the board and the next most valuable after the King. Only trade your Queen for another Queen, two rooks, or a Checkmate.

Rook	♜	5 pts.	The **Rook** is the next most valuable because of how much space it can cover. It's especially strong in the endgame.
Bishop	♝	3 pts.	The **Bishop** is a great piece that can stretch across the board.
Knight	♞	3 pts.	The **Knight** is my personal favorite. Technically, it's equal in value as the Bishop, but the Knight is tricky and can win you free pieces.
Pawn	♟	1 pt.	The **Pawns** are the workhorse of your Chess army. You can trade a Pawn for any other piece, and don't be shy about trading it for position early in the game. In the endgame, however, the Pawn's value skyrockets (more on this later).

WHY YOU WANT TO KNOW THE VALUE OF EACH PIECE

In Chess, you can't simply keep all your pieces safe and sound til the end of the game. Luckily, it's not like the first Harry Potter where Ron will die if he's taken by another piece. If you want to win, you're going to have to trade. And to make good trades, you have to know what each piece is worth.

How is the value of the piece going to influence your trading?

First, when you're considering a trade, it's not always as simple as a Bishop for a Bishop. Sometimes you actually have to do the math when trading, say, a Queen for two Rooks.

Second, even when you're considering an equal trade. It's good to know how many total points each opponent owns. If your opponent owns more total points, you want to avoid equal trades. Personally, I like trades where my opponent loses points (cue nefarious pipe organ music).

PART 2: TRADE ALL THE WAY DOWN

Once you have more points than your opponent, you can make equal trades all day. I see a lot of beginners try to save every single piece. Don't do this! If your opponent accidentally sacrifices her Knight, Bishop, Rook, or Queen, you now have a significant edge in points. Now you can **Trade All the Way Down.**

What is Trading All the Way Down? Let's say your opponent accidentally gives you her Rook. That's worth 5 points! If you trade your second Rook for her second Rook, your Bishop for her Bishop, your

Bishop for her Knight, your Knight for her Bishop, your Queen for her Queen, and so on. You're still ahead by a *whole Rook!*

That's Trading All the Way Down: When you're ahead, make equal trades until most pieces are gone from the board and you're still ahead by one piece. Now, she has fewer pieces to protect her King. The game will shortly end in your favor.

Moral of the story, don't try to save every single piece. That's just more risk that you will make a mistake and lose your edge. Once you're ahead, **Trade All the Way Down.**

PRINCIPLE #3: THE WEAPONS OF CHESS

If you went to war tomorrow, would you rather have a tank or a pistol? These are your weapons of attack. And they can be harder to learn. But if you learn how to use them and you start looking for them in your Chess games, you will conquer.

In the example above, I mentioned that if your friend *accidentally* gives you his Rook then you can **Trade All the Way Down**. What if you could *take* his Rook and not lose a piece of your own? Well, you could still **Trade All the Way Down**.

That's what **Forks, Pins, and Skewers** achieve. When executed correctly, they give you a *huge* lead for nothing. Let's talk about Forks first since they're my favorite.

FORKS

A **Fork** is when a Knight, Bishop, Rook, or Queen attacks two pieces on different squares at the same time. In the **image below**, a Knight has forked a Queen and a Rook. Notice the "fork" shape the arrows make.

The opponent can move either the Queen or the Rook, but he can't move both! You'll notice that the Queen and Rook are protecting each other, but it doesn't matter. You remember that the value of a Queen is 9 points and a Rook is 5 while a Knight is only 3 points. So, White will gladly make that trade any day.

While my favorite piece to fork with is the Knight. You can also fork with Bishops, Rooks, and Queens. Here are a few examples.

A Bishop Forks two Rooks.

A Rook forks a Knight and Bishop.

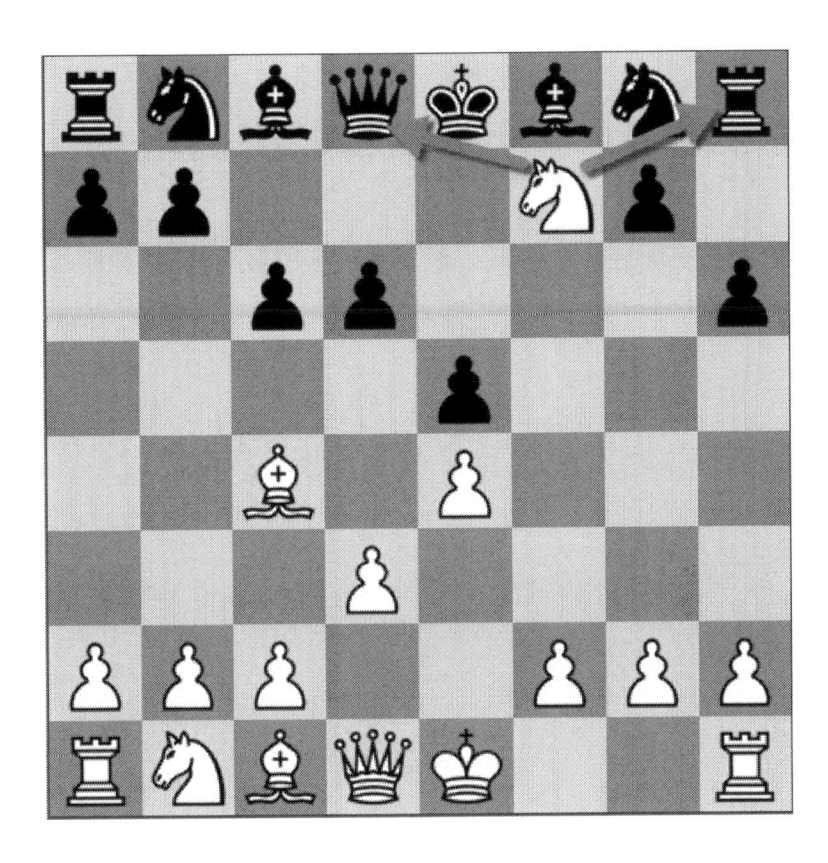

A Knight forking a Queen and Rook.

In the **picture above**, notice the King can't take the White Knight because the Bishop protects it. From the beginning of the game, I am trying to put my Knight in this position. The game is in my favor from here on out.

PINS

A **Pin** is when your piece traps (or pins) your opponent's piece between it and the opponent's King. In the example below, Black's Rook would love to move down and eat up the White Queen, but it can't because moving down would put the King in Check, which is illegal. The Rook is pinned. Since two pieces are attacking that square, White's Queen can move up and take the Rook. Since the Black King can't attack back, White takes a free piece. Oh yeah!

148

SKEWERS

A **Skewer** is when your piece attacks two opponent pieces through each other. **See the image below**. The difference between a skewer and a pin is that the Queen in this situation is not pinned to the Rook. It *can* move and if your opponent is smart, he *will* move it. But one of those pieces is going to die. It's called a Skewer because it's like a shish-kebab that skewers through two pieces of grilled chicken.

Bishop skewers Black King and Rook

149

DISCOVERED CHECK

A **Discovered Check** is not technically a Fork, Pin, or Skewer, but it's in the same family of awesome moves and I wanted to share it with you because it's just as powerful. I also call it the **Peekaboo Maneuver**. Discovered Check is when a piece that could attack the opponent's King is blocked by one of your own pieces. When you move the blocking piece out of the way, your opponent **discovers** he's in check. In the **picture below**, the White Rook is pointed toward the Black King, but White's own bishop blocks it.

Rook is pointed toward Black's King, but is intentionally blocked by his own Bishop.

151

Peekaboo! White takes advantage of Discovered Check, attacking the Queen while the King must move out of check.

In the next picture, White's Bishop is moved out of the way. Notice that the Rook is putting the King into check and the Bishop is attacking Black's Queen. Since the King must move out of check immediately, White's Bishop can take Black's Queen for free. Booyah.

If you want to pull ahead in points, **Forks, Pins, and Skewers**, and **Discovered Check** are the best way to do it. In order to incorporate them into your repertoire you'll have to actively look for opportunities to use them. But I promise, once you got it, it's like bringing a laser gun to a knife fight.

PRINCIPLE #4: CASTLE EARLY, CASTLE OFTEN

Did you know there are three *special* moves in Chess? Most novices don't know about them. In fact, if you do one of them, most novices will think you're cheating and you will have to prove to them they're real. One of those moves is **Castling** and it's one of the most important moves you can do.

Castling is when, after you have **cleared the pieces between a King and a Rook**, and you have moved **neither the King nor the Rook**. You can move the **King two spaces** toward your Rook of choice, and move the **Rook to the other side of the King** in a single turn.

What!?

Yeah. It's real. Here's a Youtube video of a very sophisticated man showing you how to castle:

> **Beginning Chess Lessons: Part 2 : What is Castling in a Chess Game** https://www.youtube.com/watch?v=nECzHBY6sEY

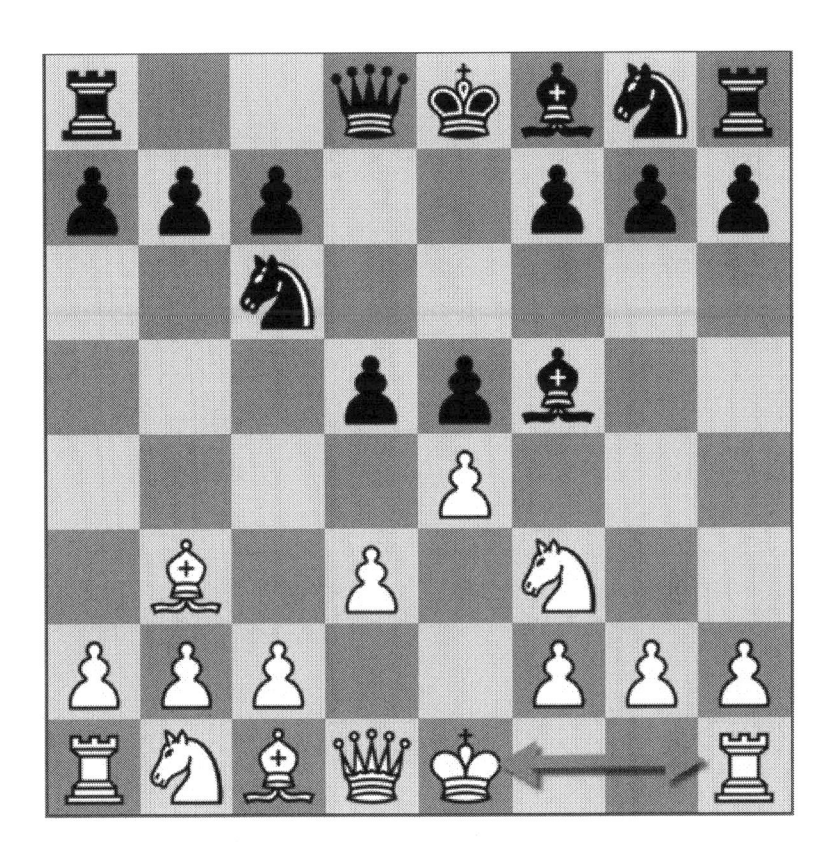

A King and Rook before Castling.

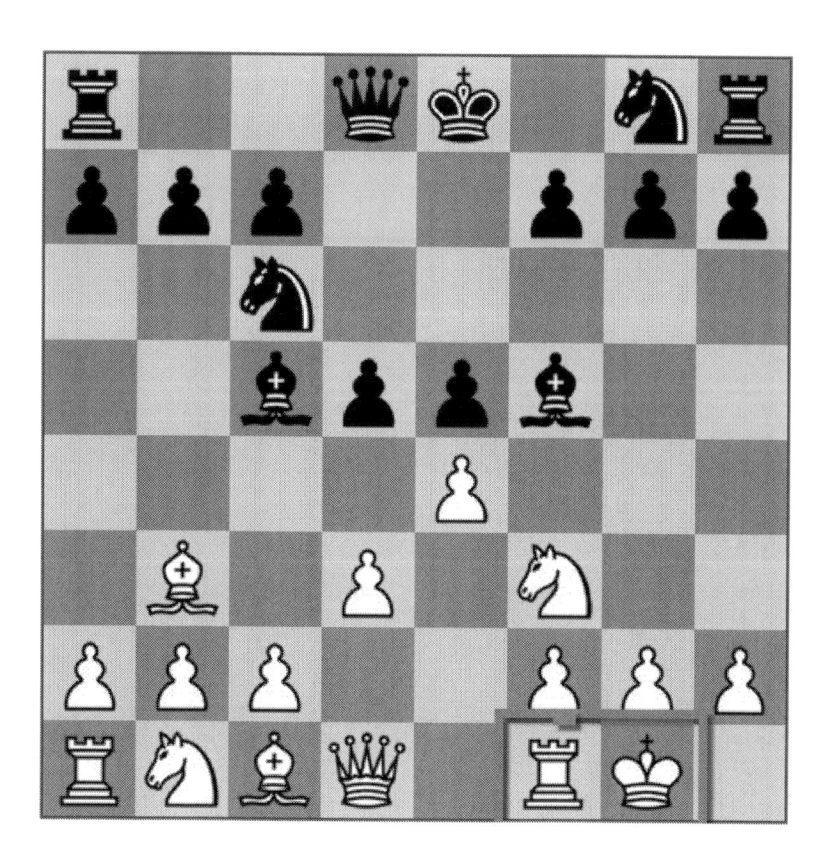

A King and a Rook after Castling

When I first used this move on my nine-year-old brother, he started to cry and exclaimed that I was cheating. That's how powerful this move is. Remember, with great power comes great responsibility.

So, why is this move one of the most important things you can learn? Here's why:

1. It blows people's minds
2. It moves your King out of the center where he is protected by Pawns
3. It releases your Rook to wreak havoc on your opponent

4. It allows you to dodge your opponent's attack

Have you ever seen a football game where a running back with the ball jukes a defender and runs ten more yards? That's what this is. It's a juke for your King. At least, that's how I thought of it before I got good.

Before I dedicated myself to getting better at Chess, I knew what Castling was, I just didn't know how or when to use it. You're going to learn right now what took me years to figure out: **Caste Early, Castle Often**

Before I knew how to Castle, I would wait until the moment my opponent was just about to launch an attack on my King. And then castled.

It sounds like a good idea, but the problem is by the time your opponent is close enough to your King to attack, he may be able to prevent you from castling. Remember that your King can't be in check, cannot pass through check, and cannot pass into check when castling. If you wait until the final moment, it may be too late. In other words, **the best time to Castle is as soon as possible. Castle Early, Castle Often.**

Instead of thinking of Castling as a defensive move, think of it as an offensive move. Castling opens your Rook to contribute to your offense. Instead of your Rook sitting in the corner until the end of the game, it's now able to protect your other pieces, and/or attack the other side of the board.

If we're thinking about it from a points perspective, you have 5 more attacking points at the *beginning* of the game. That's huge. If the god of Chess floated down from the sky and said to you, "take this powerful extra piece that you can use in the beginning of the game," and handed you a Rook, you'd take it.

Now, you can still use it as juke for your King if you have to, but if you want to utterly destroy your friends in Chess...**Castle Early, Castle Often.**

PRINCIPLE #5: KEEP YOUR QUEEN BACK

Many novices know about this. It's one of the first things you learn when you formally take on Chess, but I'm including it here because it's one of the most important things you will *ever* learn in Chess....and possibly in life. **Do not move your Queen!**

Okay, you remember that, right? Good. Now I'm going to modify that statement. **Do not move your Queen...*until your other pieces are developed.* Keep your Queen Back.** You knew it was coming because you've moved your Queen before and the Chess police didn't come to arrest you. But when you move beyond the beginner level of Chess, you'll want to keep your Queen back. The reason you want to keep your Queen back is:

1. Your Queen protects your King
2. Your Queen protects your center Pawns (which control the center. See principle #1)
3. Your Queen is your most powerful piece (if you lose it at the beginning, you're screwed)
4. If you move your Queen too early, you lose critical time to develop your other pieces

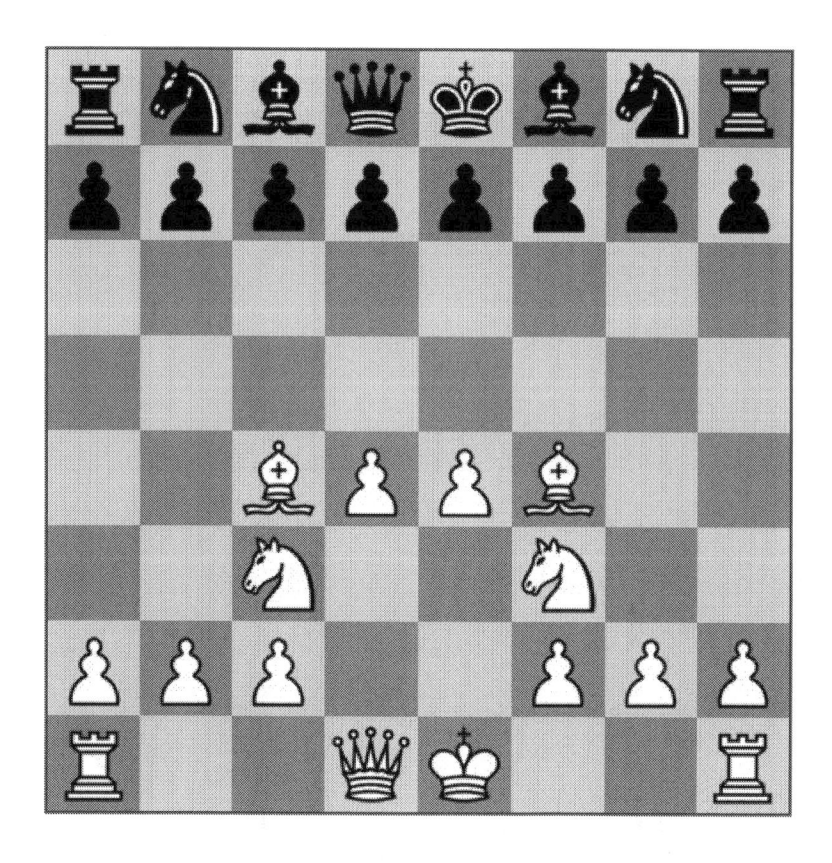

The picture above shows all of the pieces after they're developed. After your pieces are developed is a good time to move your Queen.

Reason number 4 is the most important. Let me tell you a little story about a kid named Eduardo.

EDUARDO

Once upon a time, I had a friend who was a teacher at a local high school. One day, this freshman named Eduardo came to my friend and

asked, "Mister, I want to start a Chess Club will you help me?" My friend Zach didn't know anything about Chess so he enlisted me and my friend Mark's aid.

The first day I met this Eduardo kid, I could tell he was exceptionally bright. But he was a cocky. He bragged about how he won a Chess tournament at school and he was the best player around. And he was the worst trash-talker. I mean, he talked trash the entire game—a Chess game! It was his dream to become a professional Chess player.

On the first day, I played against him and what did he do? He tried to 3-move Checkmate me! He pulled his Queen out first chance he got! Well, I'm no pro, but I know how to shut down a 3-Move checkmate, so I shut it down. But he kept moving his Queen around and I'm sad to say eventually he won.

I'm not gonna lie. He was good at thinking ahead, if only with his Queen.

The next week we played, and he tried it again. By that time, I knew his game. And I knew enough to know that pulling your Queen out early is a bad idea, so I used it against him. I developed my pieces normally and attacked his Queen whenever I could, which forced him to move his precious Queen and lose a turn. Of course, he lost.

At the end of the game, I said, "You know, Eduardo, if you keep your back Queen until you've developed your pieces, you might win more." But of course, he shrugged it off and mumbled, "I win all the time with my Queen."

He kept playing me, and week after week, he kept losing. One day he got so upset he couldn't win that he nearly started crying. Through his shaky voice, he said he wasn't sure if he wanted to play Chess anymore and asked himself out loud how I was beating him when he was a way better player. And I gently reminded the little punk, "If you just keep your Queen back, I promise you'll win more."

The next week, he tried it. He didn't win the first time. His entire strategy was based on a 3-move checkmate, so he didn't know how to develop his pieces normally. So, he asked me, "What am I supposed to do if I don't use my Queen?"

Aha! This was the defining moment. I showed him how to develop his pieces and convinced him to base his strategy around controlling the center, using forks, castling early, and keeping his Queen back!

The next week he came back with a vengeance. He used the strategies I taught him and he started winning. And winning. And winning. That was the information he needed to soar. After that, I didn't beat Eduardo too often. We found him a new instructor at a higher level and he continues to improve today.

I'm still not sure if I did a good thing helping Eduardo, but the point of the story is if you choose to take your Queen out, your total reign over your friends may be short.

PRINCIPLE #6: WIN THE QUEEN RACE

We've all been there. You're at the end of the game. There are only a few pieces left on the board. You're trying to checkmate your opponent, but you just. Can't. Trap him. His King is running around the board like a chicken with its head cut off, but you can't narrow him down. The end of the game goes for another half hour before you finally just call it a draw.

This part of the game is called the Endgame. As you may or may not know, there are three parts of chess. The Opening, the Middle Game, and the Endgame. It's important to know strategies for all three.

Here, we're going to cover what is, in my opinion, the most important Endgame strategy: **Win the Queen Race.**

The Queen Race starts like this: You're near the end of the game. You probably traded all the way down. You each have a Bishop and a Rook and there are a few Pawns on the board. No one has any immediate means of checkmating the other. What do you do?

Remember Principle #1 when I said to control the center? Forget *that* for the rest of the game! It's time to shift your entire focus to Promoting a Pawn to a Queen!

What!?

That's right. You know how a Pawn is the diddly guy who can't do much except move one space forward and can't even move backward? At the end of the game, that diddly little guy is your HERO because if you move him to your opponent's edge of the board, you can promote him to a Queen!

Remember how we talked about Castling as one of three special moves in chess. Promoting is one of those three special moves and it will save your butt if you prioritize it. Check out this video that will show you what promoting a Pawn to Queen looks like:

What Is Pawn Promotion? | Chess
http://youtu.be/Ulb1UiD4cMY

You can promote to any piece you want (except a Pawn or a King), but 90% of the time, you want to promote to a Queen. It's like one day at work you're a mail clerk and the next day you're the Senior Vice President!

So, how does one go about promoting a Pawn to a Queen? You'll want this Pawn to be the best qualified candidate before you decide to promote him. The following is a list of qualifications you'll want him to have in the order you'd want.

> **First,** find a Pawn that is further ahead than the other Pawns. The ideal candidate is the Pawn that is furthest toward your opponent's edge.
>
> **Second,** find a Pawn that has no other Pawns or pieces in front of him (in his column).
>
> **Third,** find a Pawn with protection from a stronger piece. Rooks are great for this. You can also use a Queen, Bishop, or Knight, to protect the square where he will eventually be promoted.
>
> **Fourth,** find a Pawn that has no enemy pieces in the column next to him. I list this one fourth because this can sometimes work to your advantage.

Fifth, find a Pawn that has a teammate Pawn in the column next to him. That way, if an enemy piece takes him or blocks his path, his Pawn teammate can either protect him or pick up the baton and run for a promotion.

The **picture above** is from an actual game where I was playing as Black. I used the criteria above to determine the Pawn in the red square is the best candidate. It was a close call between this pawn and the pawn slightly ahead of him, but ultimately this one was the better choice because

1. there are no enemy pawns in the column next to it,
2. there are no enemy pawns in front of it

165

3. the Queen can easily protect the square where my Pawn will be promoted.

Notice that White has equal pieces as me, but White eventually loses because I manage to promote my Pawn to a Queen and White does not have a clear path to promote either of his pawns.

There are probably a hundred different strategies and scenarios you could learn to reinforce this concept. But if you remember one thing, it's this: **do everything you can to promote that Pawn!**

On the flip side, you also want to do everything you can to prevent your enemy from promoting his or her Pawn. Remember, it's a race. The first person to promote his Pawn to a Queen wins. You *must* **Win the Queen Race. The sooner you shift your focus, the more likely you are to win.** If your enemy gets a Queen before you do, it's off with your King's head!

PRINCIPLE #7: FIGHT FOR A STALEMATE

Speaking of endgame strategy, **Stalemate** is an extremely useful tactic that most novices have heard of, but don't know how to use to their advantage. Hopefully, by following the previous six principles, you won't need this tactic, but if you know you're not going to win, this is your next best bet. Let's start with a definition:

> **Stalemate** is when one player is not in check and cannot move ANY available pieces without putting his or her own King into check.

If you're new to Chess, you may or may not remember that it's illegal to move your own King into check. What a pain! But in this principle, we're going to use that fact to our advantage.

Stalemate occurs most often when one player only has his King and the other player has more powerful pieces. Let's say, for example, that you made some bad choices and you have no pieces left except your King. Your opponent's King, Queen, and Rook are still on the board. Well, your opponent is definitely going to win, right?

Wrong!

An almost empty board is a dangerous place for your opponent because your opponent often won't notice the squares his pieces are covering. Now's the time to **Fight for a Stalemate.**

Before I go on, let me explain *why* you would want your opponent to stalemate you. Many people think that a stalemate is a tie and the person with the most pieces wins. That is incorrect. In most circles, a stalemate means no one wins and you and your opponent don't gain or lose rating points. If you were about to lose, that's pretty good! It's not as good as winning, but it's not as bad as losing!

And let's not forget it deprives your opponent bragging rights. For the aggressor who should have won, a stalemate is embarrassing; if he had been more careful, he could have won and gained all the glory associated with it.

In the **picture below**, the White King is in stalemate. The colored squares represent the coverage by the Black Queen and Rook. Notice that the White's King is not on that coverage but also can't move anywhere.

Since White's King cannot move into check and cannot move onto any of the adjacent squares, and there are no other White pieces on the board, it's a stalemate! The game is over and nobody wins.

In the **video below**, the same dignified man will show you what a stalemate is.

> **Beginning Chess Lessons: Part 2 : What is a Stalemate in a Chess Game?**
> https://www.youtube.com/watch?v=4SMfknyjPxc&index=3&list=PL3xEMsX_i6vFPsUh_tSLLt3kAf70IZqea
>
> Here's another example:
>
> **Stalemate in chess**
> https://www.youtube.com/watch?v=cffkAasaZZg&index=4&list=PL3xEMsX_i6vFPsUh_tSLLt3kAf70IZqea

Now that you have a clear idea of what stalemate is. How do you go about it? There are a hundred million ways that a stalemate could occur, but here are a few tips you can use to get your opponent to stalemate you.

1. **Don't give up!** - If there aren't a lot of pieces left in the game, you're more likely to get stalemated. Fight it out to the bitter end.
2. **Sacrifice the Others** - Move your King into a position where he is not checked and can't move anywhere, then sacrifice your other pieces. http://www.chess.com/blog/coolthing/how-to-stalemate-yourself
3. **Repetition of Moves** - If the exact same position occurs more than three times, you can claim a stalemate.

4. **50 Moves Rule** - If both sides make 50 moves without moving a Pawn or making a capture, a player can claim a draw.
5. **Draw by agreement** – Ask your opponent if he's ready to call it a draw. If you both agree, time to play again.
6. **Insufficient Mating Material** – See below.

INSUFFICIENT MATING MATERIAL

This advice could save hours of your life. There are certain piece combinations that simply cannot result in a checkmate. Therefore, they must be stalemate. If any of the following combinations occur, you can claim a draw.

1. King vs. King
2. King vs. Bishop and King
3. King vs. Knight and King
4. King vs. Two Knights and King

If you have any of the above combinations, go ahead and call a draw.

ON THE OFFENSIVE

If you're on the offensive side of a potential stalemate, you can do a few things to make sure your opponent doesn't rob you of your glory.

1. **Visualize the squares your pieces are covering**—even your inactive pieces—otherwise you might put him in stalemate without realizing it.

2. **Check the King every time.** If you constantly put him in check, he can't be stalemated.
3. **Give him a way out.** Check that he has an available square to move to before you move. If he has a place to move, he's not going to be stalemated.
4. **Don't kill the (whole) kingdom.** In the end of the game, you might feel compelled to take all his other pieces before you checkmate him. Don't! Leave one non-threatening piece alive. If there's a piece he can move, he can't be stalemated.

Of course, stalemate is largely in the hands of the aggressor. You *will* have to fight for it. But if you're trying to get stalemated and he's not even thinking about it, you have a major advantage.

PRINCIPLE #8: WATCH FOR THE WEAK BACK RANK

Many beginners have an opportunity in front of them they don't see. Watching beginners play, I just want to scream Back Rank! Of course, I don't. But, if I did, it would probably teach them something.

A **Weak Back Rank** occurs frequently in beginner games and it's super easy to exploit if you can recognize it.

This is what you look for. **(See image below)** It's near the end of the game. Most of your opponent's pieces are gone. The opponent's King is on the farthest row. (A row is called a Rank in Chess terms). In front of the Black king, protecting him, are three Pawns. You're playing White. What move would you make?

What move would you make?

Hint: You can checkmate in one move.

In the **image above**, the pawns protecting the Black King are also trapping him! If you know how to recognize this it's the easiest checkmate you'll ever get. All you need to do is find a way to move your Rook to the back rank. **Boom!** Checkmate.

And that's why you **Watch for the Weak Back Rank.** Check out this video illustrating the back rank concept.

Chess Puzzle: Back Rank Mate
https://www.youtube.com/watch?v=2I2TDnXVavc

As you can see from the video, a back rank mate is not always as simple as moving one piece, but recognizing a weak back rank can easily win or lose you the game.

If it's *your* King that's in the back with three pawns in front, you can avoid getting back ranked in a few ways. First and foremost, make sure that you have an escape route. That is, move one of your Pawns up so that your King can duck between a triangle of Pawns to protect himself. Otherwise, make sure you have strong pieces in the back protecting your King.

Of course, there are many variations to the Back Rank. But deftly applying the principle in a game will downright mystify your friends.

8 PRINCIPLES CLOSING

There they are, eight principles you can use to conquer your friends. I guarantee that if you learn these and know them well, your Chess game will improve dramatically. You won't have to spend hundreds of dollars getting Chess lessons. You won't have to scour Youtube looking for decent Chess videos. And you won't have to learn complex Chess notation trying to learn it.

While I isolated the eight most critical things you need to know, obviously there's still so much more. If you're an absolute beginner and you've either just learned Chess or only played a few years, your first step is to just play. Play as many games as you can and do post game evaluations.

The biggest part of learning in the early stages of Chess is just getting into the habit of thinking 3 moves ahead, checking that you're not accidentally sacrificing your pieces, protecting your pieces, predicting your opponent's strategy. Those skills mainly come from concentrated practice.

From here, the things you need to know are not so easy. While I'm not an expert, I can direct you toward a few things you need to learn.

1. **Learn an Opening**

There are hundreds of openings out there. Find one White and one Black that appeal to you and learn them. Memorize the first 3 moves so that you can easily play them without thinking. You're also going to want to know different variations on the same opening so that, just in case your opponent throws out something crazy, you can adjust.

If you're interested in learning more about Openings, check out my new book: Conquer your Friends with 4 Daredevil Openings. It's easy but powerful openings for Casual Players and Post-Beginners.

2. Learn a few Mating Patterns

I'm not talking about the mating patterns of the Blue Chested Sparrow on Discovery Channel. I'm talking about common ways that you can Checkmate your opponent. You already know one, the Back Rank Mate.

3. Learn Tactics

This one's harder. There are probably thousands of tactics to learn and the conditions when you will need to use them are harder to recognize, but there are definitely times when I was playing a game and remembered a tactic I learned.

4. Learn more at the theskillartistsguide.com

Of course, I would have loved to cover everything in this book. But my promise to you is to deliver what I think is *the* most important. On my website, I'm going to be posting articles for readers covering a few of the tactics that support the 8 principles in this book. Check it out! And if you like to express yourself through learning new skills, you may enjoy future articles. Get on the list!

CHAPTER 4: TIPS TO ACCELERATE YOUR LEARNING

I've already showed you the principles that will help you improve your Chess game. Here are a few Skill Artist tricks that can help you get better faster.

1. Play Faster

Hands down, my Chess game improved the most when I started playing faster. Originally, I was a very slow Chess player. Now I frequently play 10 minute blitz games.

I discovered when I started playing faster that I actually made *less* mistakes. Having more time did not improve my game, and to this day, more than 10 minutes on my clock does not lead to better choices.

If you're typically a slow player, I would advise playing 40 minute games (20 minutes for each player) to start out. Then, work your way down to 20 minute games. The idea is to play faster than you are comfortable. Pretty soon you'll be comfortable and you'll have to play even faster.

The advantage of playing faster is it forces you to *know* your technique before you move. Having excess time can actually lead to **Decision Fatigue**, which often results in poorer choices later in the game, especially for newer players. Also, the faster you play, the more games you play, and having played more games can give you a better perspective of the middle game and endgame.

On the other hand, I once saw a pair of new players playing very fast. At first, I was impressed...until I saw they were sacrificing their pieces with bloody reckless abandon. So, if you tend to be a fast player, but make a lot of mistakes, try slowing down for a while until you've internalized basic chess and the 8 principles I listed above.

In order to play faster you'll need a Chess Clock. If you play live Chess on Chess.com it automatically clocks your time. Here are a few other free or low-cost choices you can use.

Computer Chess Clock

Here's a Free Chess Clock you can run from an Internet browser: http://www.online-stopwatch.com/chess-clock/

Chess Clock App for iPhone or Android

These days I would recommend getting an App for your phone. It's the least expensive option and it usually works the best. My favorite Chess Clock App is by Chess.com. It's free and you can find it in the App store. Just go to the app store and search Chess Clock App.

Physical Chess Clock

You can also buy a physical Chess Clock. For some reason, Chess Clocks are heinously expensive. They range from $20 to $70. If it's twenty dollars or less it will probably break within a few months, so I would recommend getting one of the nicer ones. Here are a few suggestions from Amazon: http://www.amazon.com/s/ref=nb_sb_noss_1?url=search-alias%3Daps&field-keywords=Chess+Clock

2. Strengthen your Chess muscle

Skill artists know that learning a new skill is like strengthening a muscle. **Repeat to Remember**. Here's how you can think of it. If you want stronger biceps, would you go to the gym, do one bicep curl and go home? No! First, you repeat it 9 more times. You do 10 repetitions again. Then again. And *then* you can move on (and hopefully work something other than your bicep, but that's another topic for a Skill Artist's Guide). And a few days later you'll come back to the gym and follow the same routine.

In order to get your brain to remember a skill long term, you must expose it to the new skill consistently for an extended period of time. For example, to learn Chess, I would say practice or play every day for at least a week. Then, you can take a couple days off. But play for another week straight after that. Continue this schedule until you've reached your goal.

Your sessions can be anywhere from 10 minutes to 3 hours. I don't recommend playing more than three hours because your brain fatigues after a while and training stops being effective. Now, if you have to take an extra day off here or there, that's okay. Everybody's schedule is different. But don't take more than a few days off because your Chess muscle will atrophy.

3. Get a Partner or Join a Community

Because humans are naturally social, the brain engages easier when there's a physical person in front of it. Find someone who is at your level or teach him a few of the principles (maybe not all of them, mwahaha) and engage him in friendly competition. After every game, I would encourage you to do a post game analysis. Discuss with your partner why you either lost or won the game. Learn from it and play again.

If you don't have a Chess partner, or even if you do, it's always good to join a community of Chess players. In most cities there are local Chess clubs, just search Google for Chess clubs in your area.

4. Join an Online Community

You can also join an online community. My biggest leaps in Chess came when I joined Chess.com. I highly recommend this site to anyone. You can join for free and play live Chess against people from all over the world. This is a great way to practice your Chess skills. They also have a program called Chess Mentor that teaches you strategy and tactics with a premium membership ($14 a month).

One of the biggest advantages of playing online is you can **Measure your Progress** by getting a rating. It's easy to think you're getting better when...actually you're not. (Trust me I'm guilty of this too.) That's why it's important to find an objective way to measure your progress so you can constantly strive for a better rating and playing online is a great way to do that.

I mentioned Chess.com has a great Chess Clock App. They also have a great general Chess App. You can play live online, learn tactics, and watch Chess videos. I also recommend the Chess with Friends app, which allows you to connect and play with your friends over the internet.

Most people have a Chess program on their computer. I don't recommend playing against a computer to learn Chess because computers don't make the mistakes humans do. You want to play against someone who is at your level and Chess computers either totally destroy you, or they make weird mistakes that don't make sense.

CONCLUSION

I can honestly say some of the best times of my life were playing Chess with my friends and family. I created this book because I wanted to help other casual Chess players engage themselves in this game and I hope that I've helped you accomplish that.

Don't stop here! Good skill artists **Find Multiple Sources**. I've included more Chess books and resources in the Resources section at the end of the book. You can also visit my website at theskillartistsguide.com. Stay in touch and subscribe because I'll be posting other Chess tactics.

While I encourage and love self-education, you can also hire a Chess tutor or join a Chess class. Skill Artists know how and when to get advice. Search google for educators in your area.

Also, **spread the word!** Comments about your experience with the book are very helpful. Share your story with us at the Skill Artist website, my facebook page, amazon.com, maxen@skillhackr.com, or any other place this book is sold.

You might have a significant edge after reading this book, but hey, there's no reason you can't share these secrets. Now is your chance to take what you've learned and give back to the community. Challenge your friends to improve. Encourage learning and progress. Teach a younger sibling how to play Chess.

Or, completely conquer your friends. Who's keeping tabs?

RESOURCES

WEBSITES

Chess.com

Free website where you can play live against people around the world. If you want to improve your Chess game. I recommend a premium membership for $14/month. They have a program called Chess mentor that teaches you everything from how to move the pieces to the most advanced moves.

www.chess.com

Chesscademy

Cool and free website that teaches you the basics through interactive Chess lessons. All the training is free.

http://www.chesscademy.com/exercises/skewer-the-shish-kebab

Velocity Chess

New website where you can play for free or win gift cards by wagering.

www.velocitychess.com

Want more?

DOWNLOAD YOUR FREE EBOOK!

Top 6 MOVES TO AVOID in the Opening

CHESS

A Cheat Sheet for Casual Players and Post-Beginners

MAXEN TARAFA

Your first 5 to 10 moves are the most critical moves in the entire game. In this **free ebook**, I show you **6 moves NOT to make** in the Opening. By simply NOT making these moves you gain a huge edge on your opponents. Join the casual Chess revolution today! Enter your email to download and receive free book offers and updates! 20 pages.

Download here

INK AND PAPER ON YOUR BOOKSHELF!

Now available in paperback!

Enjoy the eBook? Know a kid who likes Chess? Studies show kids and teens prefer ink-and-paper books. If you enjoyed the eBook or you want to share this book with someone you know, buy the paperback version.

Click Here to Buy Paperback Version!

MORE WAYS TO CONQUER YOUR FRIENDS!

Now Available!

If you liked this book, you may enjoy the next installment in the Conquer your Friends series: You know you need to control the center, but exactly how do you do it? Answer: An Opening. Learn the exact moves to control the center, steal your opponent's pieces, and even checkmate your opponent with your first 5 moves.

Click Here to Buy eBook or Paperback from Amazon

CHESS OPENINGS:

CONQUER YOUR FRIENDS WITH 4 DAREDEVIL OPENINGS

BY MAXEN TARAFA

www.theskillartistsguide.com

Chess Openings: Conquer your Friends with 4 Daredevil Openings
Copyright © 2015 by Maxen Tarafa
All rights reserved. This book or any portion thereof
may not be reproduced or used in any manner whatsoever without the
express written permission of the publisher except for the use of brief
quotations in a book review.
www.theskillartistsguide.com

CONQUER YOUR FRIENDS WITH 4 DAREDEVIL OPENINGS

FOR CASUAL PLAYERS AND POST-BEGINNERS

Chapter 1: Chess Openings...The Skill Artist Way

Chapter 2: How to Learn from this Book

Chapter 3: What is an Opening and Why You Need One

Chapter 4: Opening Principles
    Principle #1: Control The Center
    Principle #2: Develop your Pieces
    Principle #3: Castle Early, Castle Often
    Principle #4: Don't Move your Queen

Chapter 5: 4 Daredevil Openings
    The Evil Knievel
    The Fried Liver Attack
    The Kamikaze Mate
    The Spanish Berzerker
    Black Openings

Chapter 6: Openings...Bringing it all Together
    Learning Openings: Step-by-Step
    Other Opening Tips

Conclusion

DOWNLOAD YOUR FREE EBOOK!

Your first 5 to 10 moves are the most critical moves in the entire game. In this **free ebook**, I show you **6 moves NOT to make** in the Opening. By simply NOT making these moves you gain a huge edge on your opponents. Join the casual Chess revolution today! Enter your email to download and receive free book offers and updates! 20 pages.

Download here

CHAPTER 1: CHESS OPENINGS...THE SKILL ARTIST WAY

CHAPTER 1: CHESS OPENINGS…THE SKILL ARTIST WAY

My name is Maxen R. Tarafa, and I'm a Skill Artist. If you're looking for safe Chess techniques you can show your teacher or your grandma, you've come to the wrong place. But if you're looking for 4 Daredevil Openings to destroy your friends in an alarmingly short amount of time, go ahead and take a seat.

In my #1 bestselling Chess book *8 Easy Principles*, I gave you 8 of the easiest and highest-impact principles you can use immediately to conquer your friends.

In this book, I'm narrowing it down even further. I'm going to show you why **an Opening is *the* singlemost important thing** you can learn to improve your game, and the **exact four opening moves I use to beat my friends.**

Before I dedicated myself to learning Chess, I thought Openings were only for "serious" Chess players. To me, Openings were hard and difficult to remember. What I didn't know was I was already using them. I was naturally developing my own "openings," they just weren't very effective because I didn't know the power of memorizing it and knowing it inside and out. It wasn't until I focused on Openings and Opening technique that I was able to burst through my learning curve.

Who is this book for? Maybe you've played Chess for years, but you know little more than how to move the pieces. Maybe you read my previous book and are looking for more ways to learn Chess fast. Or maybe you feel good about your Chess ability and you just need a good opening. (You don't need to have read 8 Easy Principles to benefit from this book.)

Whether you're new to Chess or you've played for years, if you know little more than how to move the pieces, this book is for you.

Honesty time.

Here's why you'll want my Chess book over others. Because I'm *not* a Chess grandmaster. I'm *not* a professional Chess player. I'm a casual player who started out as a fledgling Chess enthusiast and learned how to destroy my friends in Chess in a fantastically short amount of time. (I went from a 600 player to a 1300 player in three months). And I want to help you do what I did, but faster.

My approach is simple. In most any skill, if you learn and apply the most critical lessons, you'll be at least twice as good as the untrained beginner. Many people in the self-development space call this the 80/20 rule. If you learn and apply the most important lessons, the other smaller lessons become a lot easier.

You see, most "experts" bombard you with every single lesson you may or may not want to know from beginning to end. My books are focused on learning fast and playing against your *friends*.

Is this cheating? A lot of "experts" would say yes.

I just call it effective learning.

I'm committed to giving you the fastest and easiest way to learn Chess ever seen. But why learn Chess fast?

Because you have things to do. You have a job. You go to school. You have homework. You have kids. You have friends. You have a *life*.

You want to be good at Chess, but you don't want to spend all your time on it.

Here's how I cut your learning time down. I don't expect you to read long lists of notation. I don't expect you to pretend you care about the historical games of Chess masters.

I show you the highest impact lessons you *need* to know using pictures and everyday language.

In this book, I'm focusing on a major pain-point for beginning players, which is the Opening. Many beginners freeze up before they even start. Many beginners know opening principles, but they waste a lot of time and energy deciding which moves to make. I was guilty of both when I first started out.

Most Chess books ask you to memorize hundreds of openings, which is very time-consuming and confusing and, frankly, more time than I want to commit as a casual Chess player.

I believe if you are a casual player or a post-beginner, you can gain a massive edge against your friends if you simply know **one** effective opening and its variations very well. If you learn one common, but effective and adaptable opening and its variations, you drastically reduce your need for learning hundreds of other openings and random tactics.

That's not to say knowing a broad range of openings and tactics isn't helpful, I'm just saying for casual players and post-beginners, your time is better spent now learning one than spreading yourself thin learning hundreds.

If you're thinking there's no way YOU can memorize 3 or more Chess moves. I promise, you can. I taught a nine-year-old one of these openings and he used it the same week to beat 16 and 17-year-olds. Plus, I show you step-by-step diagrams of exactly what you need to do. Plus, plus, I'm going to show you how you can easily memorize *any* Chess opening. You can have the opening of your choice memorized with practice in 5 minutes.

I'm going to show you 4 of the exact openings I used to rapidly gain 700 points and stomp my friends. But these aren't just any openings, these are openings that are risky and sometimes shatter the rules, but *because* of that, they give YOU control of the game.

In other words, I'm giving you openings a daredevil would use… dangerous openings.

But always remember…with great danger comes great responsibility. I trust that you'll use them wisely.

Sincerely,

Maxen R. Tarafa

CHAPTER 2: HOW TO LEARN FROM THIS BOOK

CHAPTER 2: HOW TO LEARN FROM THIS BOOK

Before we launch into the openings, let's talk about how you can get the most from this book. I want to provide you the quickest, and most effective ways to learn Chess ever. So, let me introduce some of the tools I'm using help you learn.

A Brief Primer on Notation

In my first book, I took a big risk and used no notation and included no games of ancient Chess masters. Same philosophy here. But...don't be scared...I'm going to provide a quick primer on Chess notation for people who want to know. I should reiterate. You don't NEED notation for this book. So, if you don't want spend time on it, you can skip to the next page.

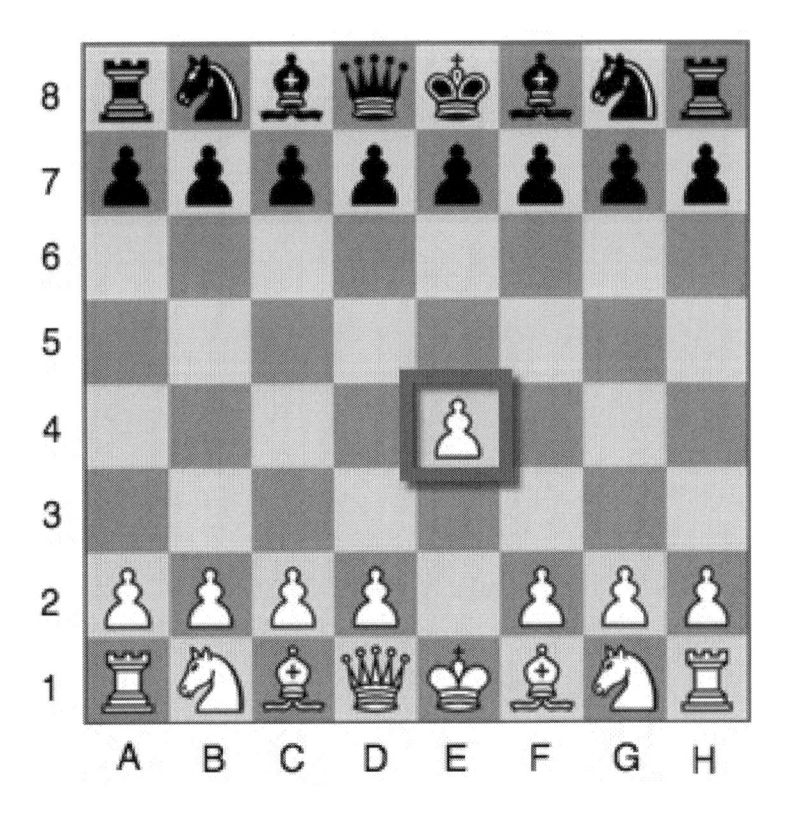

In notation, a column is called a **File**. The Files are lettered **A through H**.

The rows are called **Ranks**. They're numbered **1 through 8**.

To find a certain square, first identify the File, then the Rank. For example, in the **image above**, the highlighted Pawn is **e4**.

If you've ever played Battleship or created an Excel document, it's a lot like that.

It's also important to know notation is always from the perspective of White. So, a1 is always White's left Rook.

You may also see me refer to a piece as Kingside or Queenside. This just means it's on the side of the King or Queen. For example, when playing White, the Kingside Bishop is the Bishop directly to the right of the King on f1. Similarly, a King Pawn is the Pawn directly in front of the King. Ditto for the Queen.

That's all you need for this book. Like I said, I'll usually use an arrow or highlight to show you what I'm talking about, but just in case it's not clear, you can make absolutely certain with the exact location.

So, let's talk about the images.

Images

When I'm explaining a Chess move or principle that I think needs an image, I'll show you something like the **following image**.

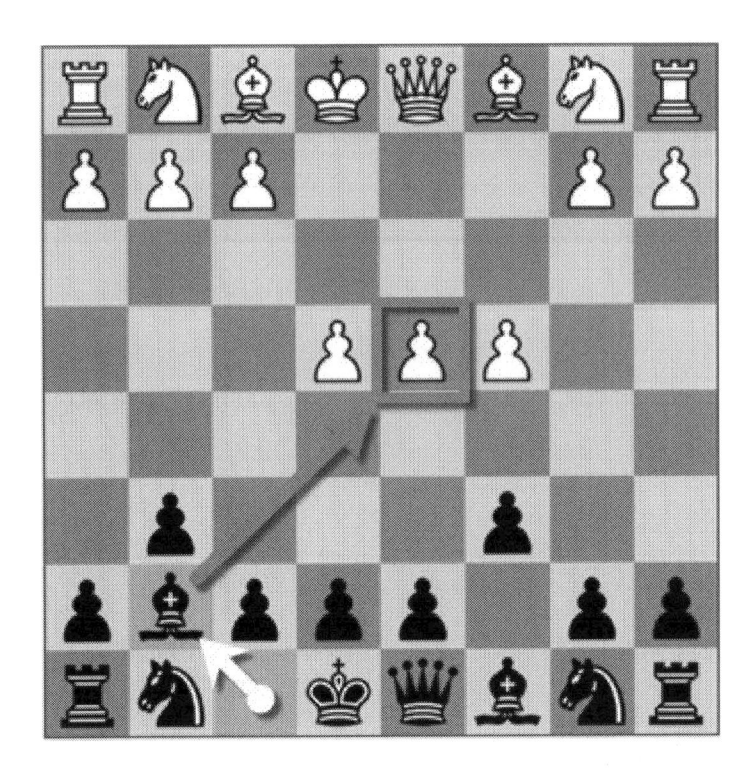

Since this book often includes a series of moves, or multiple pieces on the same image, I'll use a caption with letter or number, such as in the **image above.** The sequence of the letters tells you the sequence of the moves or the topics.

More often, you'll see red or dark grey arrows and highlights depending on your device.

Red/Dark Grey Square – Highlights the key point

Red/Dark Grey Arrow – Attacking Arrow – Shows where a piece is attacking

White Arrow – Shows where a piece came from in the previous move. I only use this if it's not obvious.

If your device is in color, you may also see a yellow square that shows where the piece came from. If your device isn't in color, don't worry about it, it may or may not be visible, but if I think you need to know where a piece came from I'll show you the White Arrow.

Links and Videos

A note on the links and videos, I use a lot of them. If your device is connected to the internet, you can just click on the link and a browser window opens. If it's not connected to the Internet, two options:

Option One: I provide the exact name of the video so you can go to Youtube and search it manually. You can type the links straight into your browser address bar.

Option Two: You can go to my website theskillartistsguide.com/chess-openings and all the videos and links will be nicely listed by Chapter on a single page and you can just click on it.

You don't have to watch every single video, but if you want to get a better idea of the principle, check it out. I realize Youtube videos probably aren't the most academically sound way to teach. But luckily, I don't care! As a skill artist, I look for clear, quality information, and if it can help me learn quickly, I use it!

Chess Experience

I'm assuming you already know how to set up the board, move the pieces, and checkmate. If you're brand new to Chess or you haven't touched a Rook in years, don't worry, you can still learn from this book, but you may want to review the basics.

Here's a link to a Youtube playlist that will teach you the basics from setting up the board and moving the pieces to checkmates.

How to Set up the Board

https://youtu.be/wH9Z1ORrtjQ

If you're a beginner, post-beginner or casual player, I highly recommend you check out my first book Chess: Conquer your Friends with 8 Easy Principles. This will give you a good overview of easy strategies beyond the basic rules. You don't *need* to read 8 Easy Principles first to benefit from this book, but, honestly, I think it will help.

Measure your Progress

If you don't have a rating yet, I would suggest that before you start learning these openings you go to Chess.com. Sign up for a free account and play Live Chess. Live Chess is cool because you can play people from across the world and even chat with them if you'd like. But the point is to get yourself a rating.

I know you mainly just want to stomp on *your* friend*s* via Chess. But the reason I say to get a rating is that you can easily accelerate your learning when you can set measurable goals and work to obtain them. If you never know where you're starting, you'll never know how far you've come, or how far you *want* to go.

Engage your Senses

As you read, you may want to play with a Chessboard next to you (especially if you're a kinesthetic learner). Or with a Chess Program (such as Chess.com) open in a separate window. It will help to practice the Openings as you go.

Alright, housekeeping is done. Let's talk about Openings.

CHAPTER 3: WHAT IS AN OPENING AND WHY YOU NEED ONE

CHAPTER 3: WHAT IS AN OPENING AND WHY YOU NEED ONE

In my first book you learned 8 easy principles to beat your friends. Now I'm going to make stomping on your friends via Chess even easier with an Opening.

But what is an Opening? A magic portal to another dimension?

Yes, but not what I'm talking about here.

When I say Opening, I'm talking your first 3 to 10 moves in every Chess game.

If you've read the first Conquer your Friends, you know the person who wins the game is often decided in the first 5 moves.

I know what you're thinking. It's five moves. Who cares?

You care. Because unlike other games, in Chess if you lose a piece or you lose board control early in the game, the effect amplifies with every move. Which means, you want to begin the game with a plan for getting ahead starting with your very first move rather than making random moves and hoping they work.

But there's another reason an Opening is important.

In Chess, you can form millions of combinations with pieces on the board. Some have said there are more Chess piece combinations than grains of sand on every beach on planet earth. When you start the game with an Opening, you're ensuring you're playing a game you're familiar with. If your friend isn't familiar with your opening (and if they're not a trained Chess player, they won't be) then you will win the opening.

Let me give you an example: I used to be an avid Super Smash Bros player. The version for N64. I was very good and I always used to beat my friend Greg.

Well, Greg was trying to get me to play the newest version of Super Smash Bros on Gamecube. He'd been playing it for like a year, but for some reason we always played the N64 version.

Well, one day he says, "why don't we change things up and play Smash for Gamecube?" And I'm thinking, it doesn't matter to me. I always win at Super Smash. It's the same game, right?

Wrong.

Greg stomped on me. Why? Same rules. Same buttons. Mostly the same characters. I should've won. But I didn't because Greg knew the nuances of the Gamecube Smash better than me. Greg had an advantage because he knew the slight changes in physics, and items, and levels better than me. He had the home court advantage.

This is like an Opening. When you use an Opening, you have home court advantage. You're playing a game you know and your friend doesn't.

Knowing an Opening has other benefits too. If you don't know what piece to move at the beginning of the game, you'll be confident you know exactly what to do. Therefore, reducing decision fatigue and giving you more brain energy for the Middle and Endgame.

Daredevil Openings

Since I want to teach you the fastest and most effective way to learn Openings, I've very carefully curated which Openings I'm going to show you. They're all Openings I've personally used and still use on a regular basis, and Daredevil Openings.

A **Daredevil Opening** is a risky Opening. It breaks the conventional rules of Chess Openings, but in return, gives you incredible payoffs.

The reason I'm showing you Daredevil Openings instead of safe ones is because daredevil openings work better for and against post-beginners. Safe openings leave too much room for variation and error, which means you'll have to rely more on memorization, patterns, and tactics.

The risky Openings work better against Post-Beginners and Casual Players because they're not prepared for them. If you use a safe opening, chance and luck gives them more of an advantage.

Do you always have to use an Opening? No. In fact, many times you won't be able to accomplish your whole opening. Other times you'll simply want to do things your own way. Which is why it's important to know Opening Principles...

CHAPTER 4: OPENING PRINCIPLES

CHAPTER 4: OPENING PRINCIPLES

I know you'd love to skip straight to those daredevil Openings, you sly dog. But before we can break the rules, we must learn them.

In *8 Easy Principles*, I briefly mentioned a few opening principles because the point was to remember it.

Now, I'm going to go into more depth about the opening principles, and how you can use those principles to your advantage.

When I show you the Daredevil Opening I personally use in the next Chapter, you'll know exactly which principles it breaks, but you'll also know which principles it uses to its advantage. If you continue to learn more Openings or you want to invent your own, these principles will show you exactly how to do it.

Let's start by reviewing the most important and most basic opening principle.

Control the Center.

PRINCIPLE #1: CONTROL THE CENTER

In the first five moves of the game, you're unlikely to take any of your opponent's pieces without losing one of your own. So, you want to fight for the next best thing: The Center. Whoever controls the center controls the game.

Just to refresh. What do I mean by the center? **In the picture below**, I've highlighted the four squares that make up the center.

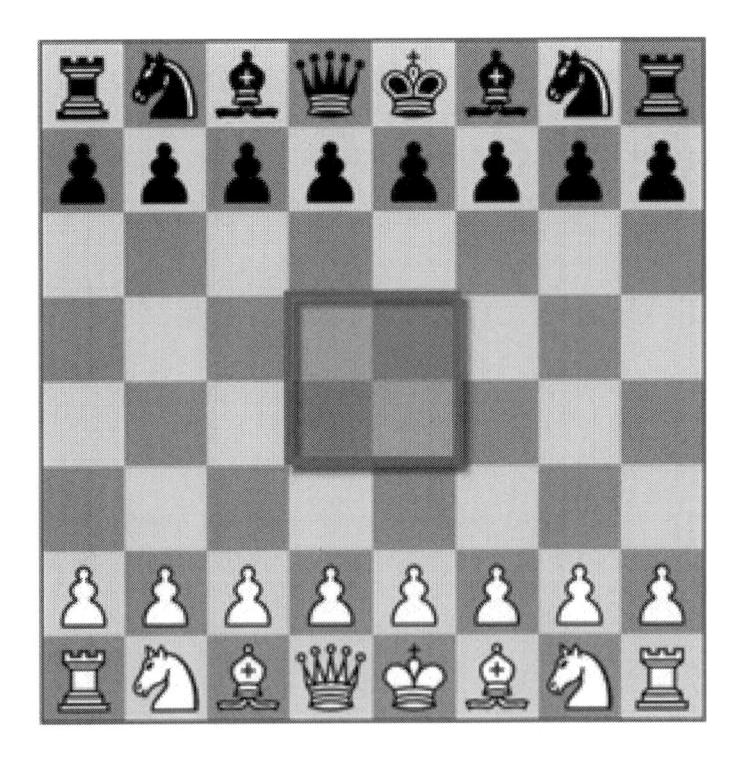

In the beginning of the game, every move you make should fight to control those four squares. Most likely your first move will be one of those center Pawns followed by your Knights and your Bishops. **In the**

212

picture below, I show what your pieces would look like if they were developed to target those four squares.

Why is it so important to control the center?

Let's use an analogy to another sport. In Soccer, have you ever seen a team fight to protect the sidelines? Have you ever seen a goalie stand in the corner of the goal while an opponent drives up the middle? I hope for your sport enjoyment's sake you have not.

Here's another analogy. In Football, your Pawns are like your Offensive line. If your Offensive line fails to control the center of the line of scrimmage, an opposing player is likely to run through and sack your Quarterback.

Center control is closely related to development. They're two sides of one coin. If you control the center, it makes it hard for your opponent to develop his pieces past the center or move his good pieces toward your King. The center is the fastest and easiest place to damage your opponent from. So, the person who controls it has far more opportunities to attack.

The **image below** shows a real beginner game where Black has firm control of the center while White has not even tried. Notice that the four squares in the middle are either taken or protected by Black.

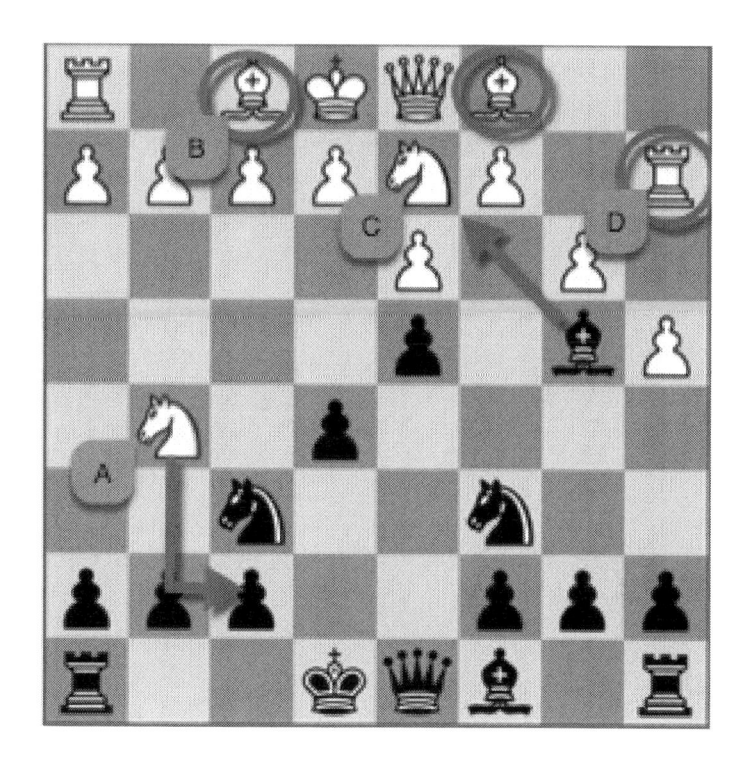

Now I'm going to show the effects Blacks' control of the center has over White.

In the **image above**, Black is dominating the center of the board. See the corresponding letters in the **image above** to get a visual of what I'm talking about:

Exhibit A: White's Knight would love to move down and gobble up Black's Pawn and Fork the Queen and Rook, but White would lose his Knight. If he had another piece to Protect his Knight (like a Bishop) he would fair much better. But since Black controls the center, White has no chance of bringing in a Bishop or any other piece.

Exhibit B: White's two Bishops **(Circled above)** are both stuck behind Pawns. White's Queenside Bishop could move down and attack Black's Bishop, but best-case scenario they would cancel each other out.

Exhibit C: White's Knight is pinned to the King, so it can't move. Again, not helping White's cause.

Exhibit D: White moves the Rook Pawns, presumably to make room for his Rook. But, all it's really done is wasted precious opening moves. His Rook is still stuck.

In summary, when you control the center, you have more moves available to you. YOU make the choices about how the game proceeds, which you can convert into winning unequal trades.

PRINCIPLE #2: DEVELOP YOUR PIECES

Developing your Pieces is moving your attacking pieces toward your enemy. In the Opening, the main pieces you want to develop are your Bishops and Knights. We develop these pieces first because they help to control the center and put pressure on the enemy camp at the same time.

Why not the Rook or the Queen? You don't want to develop your Rooks or your Queen in the Opening for two reasons: First, they're too valuable to develop first. If you move your Queen out or somehow manage to move your Rook out, you'll spend the Opening trying to defend them instead of developing your other pieces and controlling the center.

In the case of your Rooks, it simply takes too long to move the pieces out of the way to develop your Rook. So, you might as well develop your Bishops and Knights first. Then you can Castle and moving your Rook is a lot easier.

Here are some sub-principles of **Developing your Pieces.**

1. **Avoid moving the same piece twice.**

Within the first 5 moves, you don't want to move the same piece twice. Every time you move a piece twice you lose an opportunity to develop your piece and your enemy has a chance to get closer.

The only time to move your piece twice is when you're going to lose the piece for no good reason. But the more you play, the less this happens.

2. **Develop your Pieces to Protect your Other Pieces**

In order to control the center, you'll want to protect the pieces that are in the Center. Remember the bullhead image I showed you in **Control the Center?** Those pieces are all protecting other pieces that are in the center AND they are protected by other pieces. That's how you ensure your opponent can't take your center pieces. It's kind've like Jenga. If you leave too many pieces dangling unsupported, your whole structure is going to come down.

3. Stay on your Half of the Board

When I show you my top secret opening, I'm going to show you how you can break this rule. But for now, just know that you want to stay on your own half of the board (the half closest to you) in the first 5 moves because that's how you're going to maintain control of the center and keep your King safe.

4. Don't block your own Pieces

If you follow the Opening I give you in the next chapter, this won't be a problem. But, it's important to know anyway. **Don't block your own pieces.**

For the same reason you need to control the center, you don't want to block your own pieces so you can develop as many pieces as possible. Of course, sometimes your opponent will FORCE you to block your own pieces. But, you certainly shouldn't do it without a fight.

5. Develop your Knights Before your Bishops

This is a rule of thumb. This principle assumes Knights are more valuable than Bishops at the beginning of the game. Knights are great in the beginning of the game because they can jump over other pieces. Since there are more pieces to jump over in the beginning as opposed to the end, this makes them more valuable. Also, Knights tend to protect Bishops and it doesn't usually work the other way around.

PRINCIPLE #3: CASTLE EARLY, CASTLE OFTEN

I go over this more in depth in 8 Easy Principles, but I want to touch on it briefly here. You want to Castle as early as possible. This opens up your Rook, Protects your King, and frees up your Queen. In general, you want to castle within the first 10 moves.

PRINCIPLE #4: DON'T MOVE YOUR QUEEN

It's important not to move your Queen. Not even one space unless you absolutely must. Moving your Queen sets you up for problems. Remember your Queen protects your King and your other pieces.

5 PRINCIPLES CLOSING

Each of these principles is a guideline to keep you on track for taking control of center and taking control of the game. There are always situations where following the guideline might not be the best thing for you. So, you must develop the experience to know when you should follow it and when you shouldn't. I highly recommend that if you're learning openings, start out by following the rules so you know what it looks and feels like. Later, you'll know when to sacrifice for the greater good.

CHAPTER 5: 4 DAREDEVIL OPENINGS

HOW TO LEARN AND REMEMBER AN OPENING

Before we cover the Openings themselves, let's talk about how to learn an Opening. I'm going to show you *my* personal method of remembering openings without notation or visual aids.

Objective

Before I start my opening, I remember my **Objective**. Usually the objective is a particular square I want to reach with a particular piece.

Next, I separate my opening into three key positions.

The Base

The Base of an Opening is usually the first three moves. (However, it could be more or less.) It's the set-up for the opening. I can reach the base of the opening about 90 percent of the time. It's early enough in the game my opponent wouldn't be able to stop me from getting there.

The Climax

The Climax is the point at which I've accomplished my objective. It's usually a Fork, Pin, or Skewer or the point where the Payoff is guaranteed, but not yet achieved.

The Payoff

The Payoff is a material or positional gain as a result of my opening. In some Openings I gain a Rook for free; in others, I force my opponent to forfeit his Castling ability. Sometimes both.

So, those are the three main parts. There are also...

Auxiliary Steps – Necessary steps between the three benchmarks.

Variations – When your opponent does something that diverts you from your plan, you switch to a **Variation**. The variation is an alternate course that usually still results in your original goal or the next best goal.

If these aren't making much sense to you now, I promise they will when I show you the openings. So, without further ado....let's talk about my signature Opening for post-beginners: What I call **The Evil Knievel.**

THE EVIL KNIEVEL

THE EVIL KNIEVEL

I learned this Opening early in my Chess journey, and I still use it today. For this opening, I'm going to show you step-by-step exactly how it works and why we're making the moves we're making. The other 3 openings are similar to this one, if not a direct variation, so by explaining this one in detail, you'll understand the reasoning behind the other three.

Now, before I show you *how* to play it. Let me tell you the advantages.

1. It's easy to remember

The **Base** of this opening is three moves forming a triangle. Remember that and the rest is easy.

2. It reduces variables

This is a great opening for post-beginners because screwing up is hard. Safer Openings rely too much on tactics. But since this one puts pressure on my opponent right away, it forces him to respond to my opening at every step, thus reducing variables.

3. It follows most opening principles

If it doesn't go exactly the way I want, it still does a good job of accomplishing the main principles: controlling the center, developing my pieces, and preparing to castle, but most importantly….

4. It's MY game.

If I start with this opening, my opponent MUST react to my game. Because I know the variations and how to react if they throw a curveball, I can predict their moves better than they can predict mine, which gives ME an advantage.

What are the potential rewards?

If it goes EXACTLY the way I want, which doesn't always happen but often does, I'll...

1. Take my opponent's ability to Castle Kingside
2. Force my opponent to move his Queen
3. Prepare myself to Castle
4. Take a Pawn and a Rook for free

You read the last one right. Now you're seeing why I like it.

Post-Beginner Psychology

Let's talk about the psychology of this Opening. The Evil Knievel is specifically targeted to play against post-beginners because post-beginners usually can't predict Knight moves, forks, or protected pieces. You'll see what I mean when I show you the Opening, but for now I promise you can stomp on almost any beginner using this Opening.

Before I show you the three moves you need to set up this opening. I want to show you my objective.

Objective

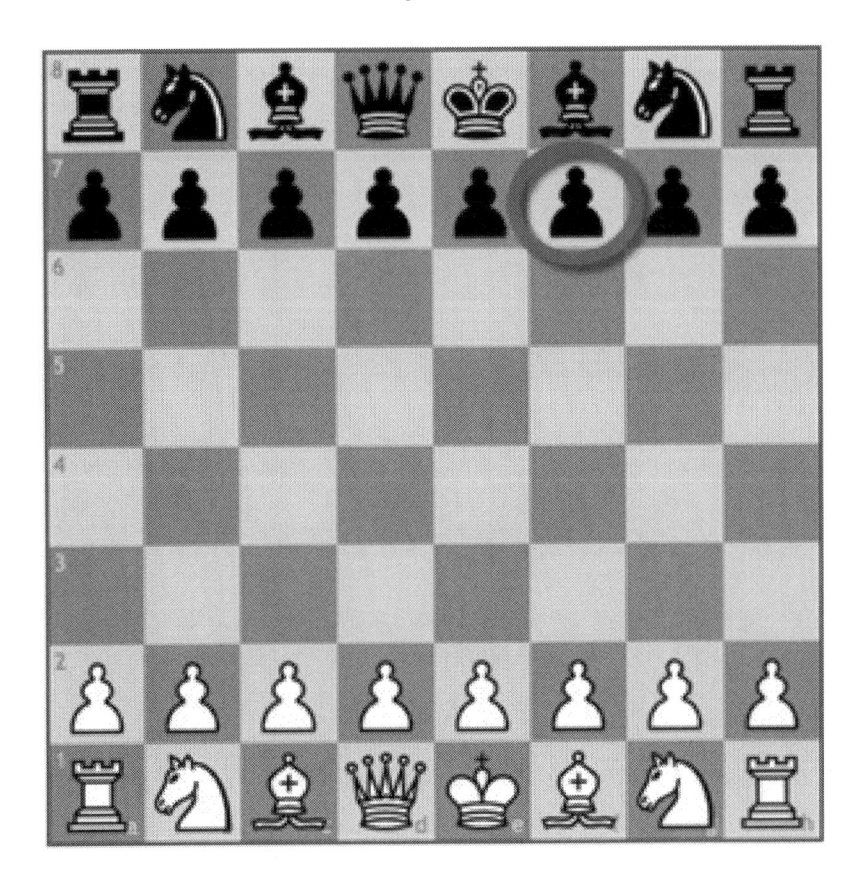

In the **image above**, I've highlighted the piece I'm targeting. My **Objective** is to put my Kingside Knight on this square. Many people call this the f7 square, since its designation in notation is f7. I call him the Footman Pawn.

Why the Footman? I've been watching this show on the BBC channel called Downton Abbey and for every lord or King there's a Footman who dresses the lord and tends to his needs. Since this Pawn usually isn't fighting the center and just sits there next to the King, I call him the Footman Pawn. See the "F" alliteration?

_F_ 7 : _F_ootman?

Back to the Opening. Before I start my opening, I always think about the square I'm targeting, his helps me remember the three moves. I only need to point my pieces at this Pawn.

Why am I targeting this pawn? What makes the f7 square so special?

I'm glad you asked. The f7 square is EXTREMELY special because it's the weakest square on the board. The only piece protecting the Footman is the King.

Ahem, that's right. The singlemost important piece on the board is the only piece protecting this Pawn. Look carefully at the picture. Even though there are other pieces next to it, only one protects it. So, if you can organize two of your pieces to attack this Pawn successfully, your chances of winning a free piece are high.

Now you know the objective. Let's get to the first move.

THE EVIL KNIEVEL
POSITION #1: MOVE YOUR KING PAWN TWO SPACES TO E4

In the **image above,** the Pawn in front of the King (often called the Kingside Pawn) is moved TWO spaces to the center. This is a common move, but it is also one of the most effective. There are two reasons why this is a great move.

First, it grabs for the Center.

Second, it opens up my Bishop *and* my Queen. Even though I don't want my Queen to move yet, I still want her ABLE to move. My Bishop is also free now, and you will see why this is important in a few moves.

THE EVIL KNIEVEL
POSITION #2: YOUR KNIGHT TO F3

In the **image above,** you notice that Black moves his King Pawn against yours. In showing you this Opening, I am showing you the MOST likely moves Black will make. Will your opponent *always* make these moves? Not always. But there's a good chance, and the good thing about this opening is if it doesn't go exactly according to plan, you can still use the same principles to play a good game.

So Black moves his King Pawn against yours and you move your Knight to f3. This is good because it still works to Control the Center. By moving your Knight to f3, you're attacking Black's King Pawn, which forces Black to make his next most likely move....

229

THE EVIL KNIEVEL
POSITION #3: BLACK KNIGHT TO C6 | WHITE BISHOP TO C4

Black moves his Knight to c6 to protect his Pawn so he can control the center. But you want to continue your attack on the Footman Pawn. Let's stop for a second a take a look at what's going on here. Your Bishop is now pointed at the Weakest Square on the board. No one has overwhelming control of the center, but you have two pieces out your opponent doesn't know are deadly.

This position is the **Base** of the Evil Knievel attack. This is what you need to remember. In case you were wondering, I call it the Evil Knievel attack because if you draw a line between my two main pieces and the piece they're attacking it forms an obtuse triangle. Kind've like a motorcycle ramp.

If you don't know who Evil Knievel is, he's a Daredevil who performed death-defying stunts by jumping his motorcycle off giant ramps (**See image above**). So, this triangle shape reminds me of the ramp.

If you remember nothing else from this entire opening, remember these three positions.

This point is pretty easy to reach. I reach the **Base** roughly 9 out of every 10 times I try it. But, this is where Black *might* throw a wrench into your plan. So, I'm going to show you how the Evil Knievel attack is *supposed* to happen.

THE EVIL KNIEVEL
POSITION #4: YOU MOVE YOUR KNIGHT TO G5

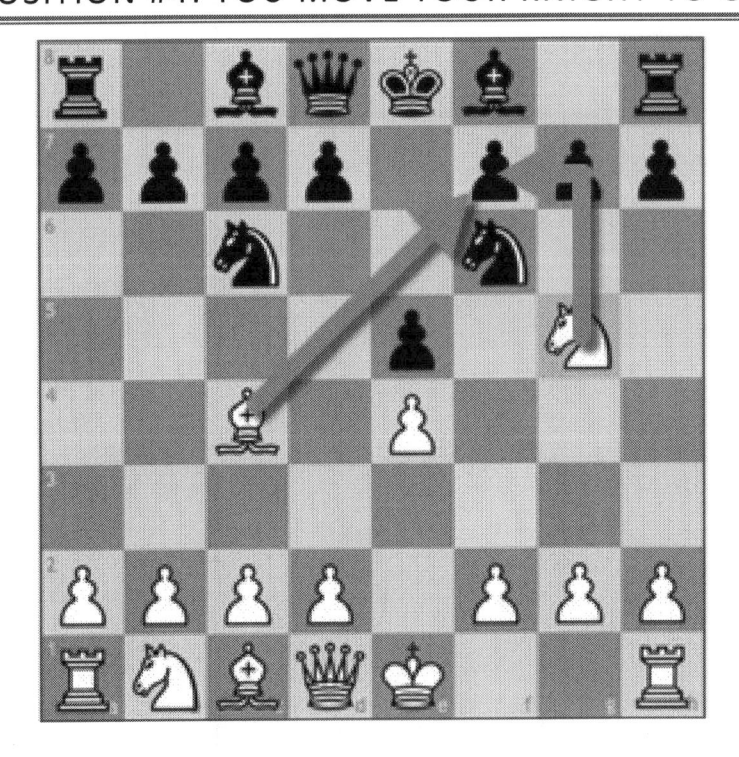

Your opponent moves his other Knight out. This Black Opening is what's called the **Two Knights Defense**. But what Black doesn't know is he's making the wrong move.

In the **image above**, you move your Knight to g5. Now, at this point, Black may or may not realize his Footman Pawn is in danger.

I'm going to argue, he's not. Why? Remember when we talked about the psychology of beginning players? Beginners typically don't predict forks, Knight moves, or protected pieces. He's probably a little nervous your Knight is on his side of the board, but he thinks all of his pieces are so close to his other pieces they're protected. So, there's a good chance, he's not even going to realize you're about to Fork him. So I'm going to show you the best-case scenario from this point.

THE EVIL KNIEVEL
POSITION #5: HE DOESN'T EVEN KNOW YOU'RE ABOUT TO FORK HIM | BLACK PAWN TO D6

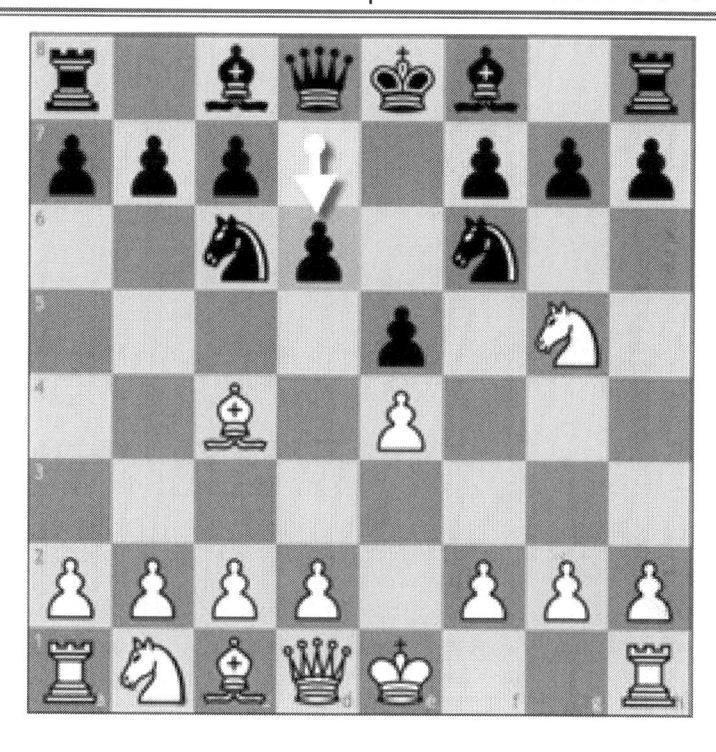

Because your opponent doesn't recognize the devious attack you're launching on him. He's probably thinking, "hmmm, he didn't do anything. Might as well support my other Pawn." So, he moves his Queen Pawn to d6. Woah, his world is about to get rocked. Because....

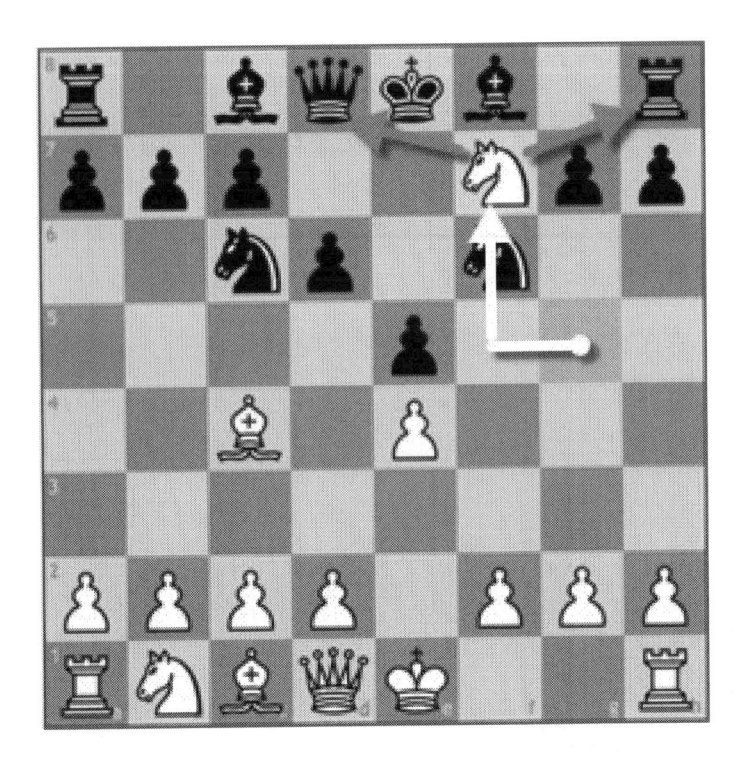

BAM! You move your Knight to f7, forking the Queen and the Rook! Here's the **Climax.** You've reached the moment you've been planning all along—your **Objective**. Most people are afraid to move their Knight to this square because it's so close to Black's pieces. But it's important to notice the King CANNOT take the Knight because your Bishop is protecting it. You're a total daredevil. Evel Knievel would be proud.

At this point, slowly but surely, your opponent is realizing, "damn, I can move either my Queen or Rook. Not both." If you're lucky, he'll move his Rook and you'll take his Queen. But let's assume he notices you're attacking the Queen….

THE EVIL KNIEVEL
POSITION #6: YOU TAKE THE ROOK.

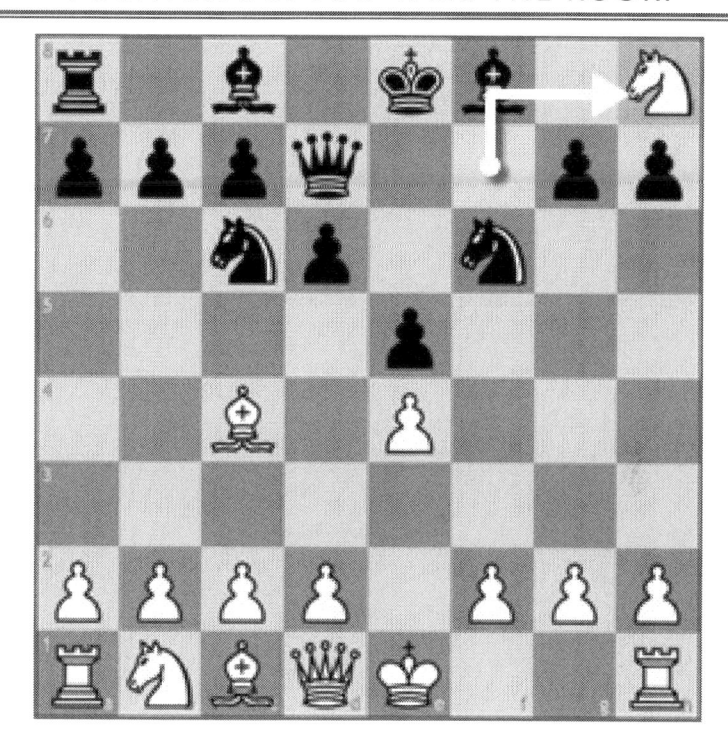

Here's the **Payoff**. He moves the Queen and you take his Rook with your Knight. That's it. It's all downhill from here. Your chances of winning are high because you're now up a Pawn and a Rook and he can't Castle Kingside. At this point, you can try and get your Knight out of there safe and sound, but usually, I pull out my Queen and castle because I know checkmate isn't far away.

From this point, you can try to extract your Knight and keep him alive, but I usually find my opponent doesn't bother to attack my Knight.

EVIL KNIEVEL: SUMMARY

You now know the Evil Knievel attack. Let's review.

Below is the **Base** of **The Evil Knievel Attack.** Each move is numbered in order of when to move it.

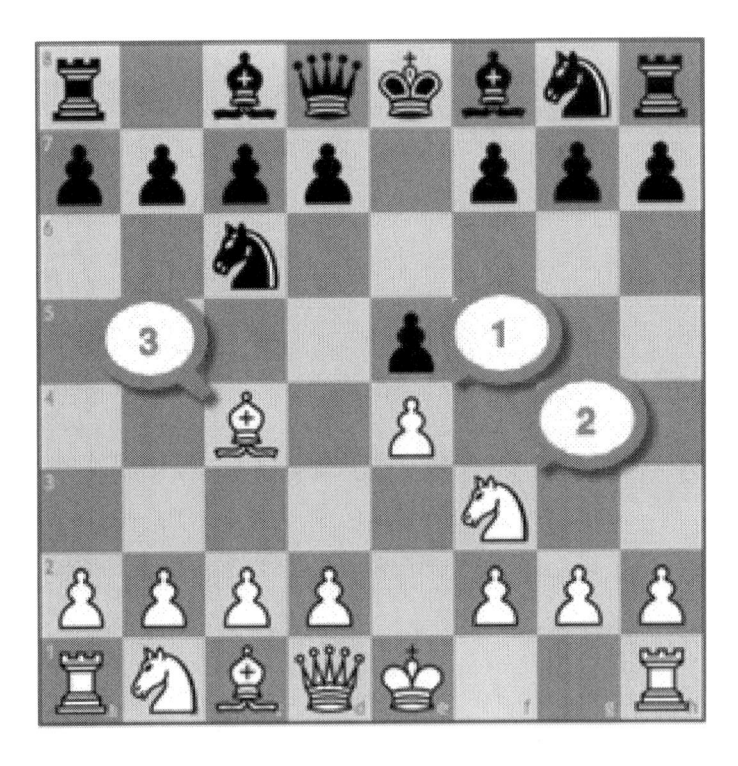

236

You can also remember it by the triangle shape it forms with the f7 Footman Pawn:

The Climax is when you take his Footman Pawn. (**Below**)

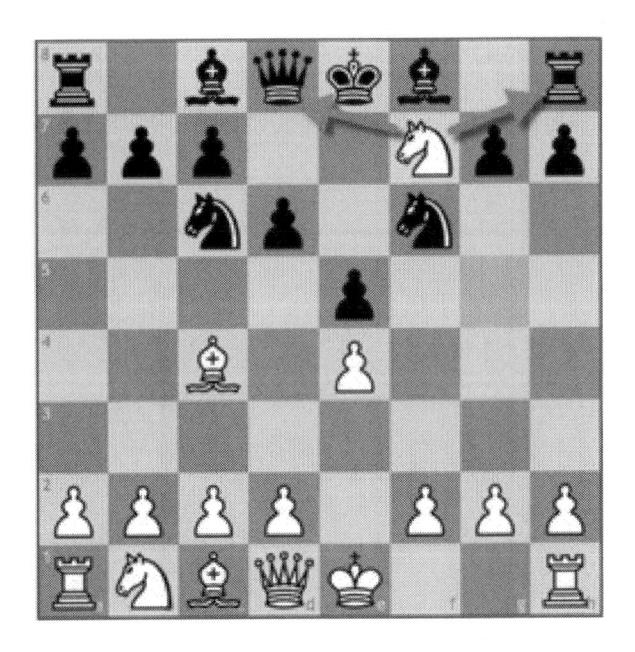

The Payoff is when you take his Rook for free. **(below)**

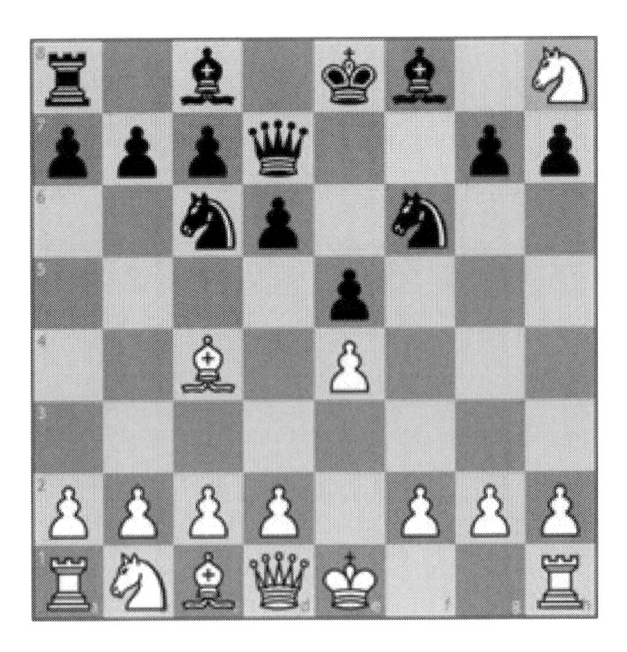

238

THE FRIED LIVER ATTACK

THE FRIED LIVER ATTACK
INTRODUCTION

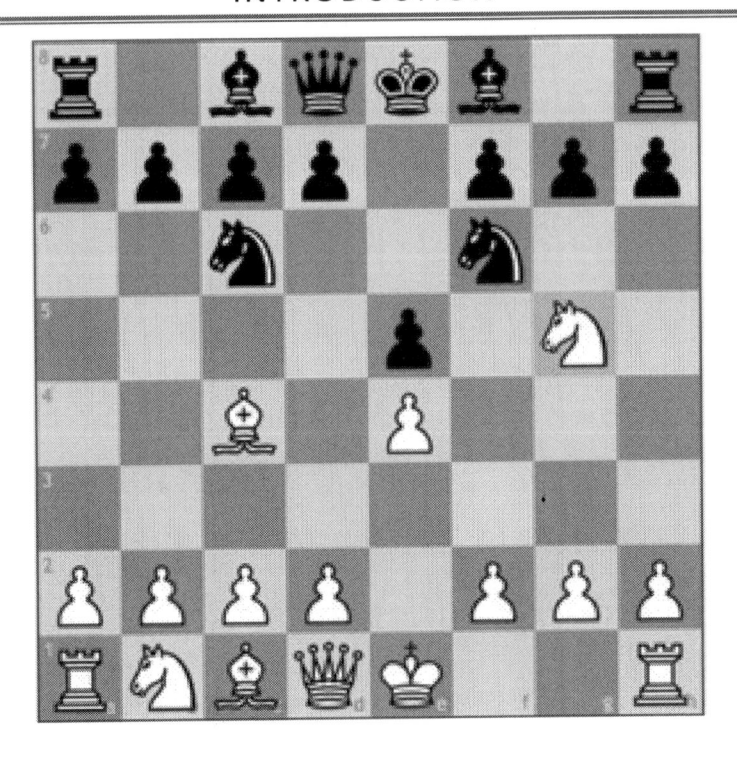

The Fried Liver Attack is very similar to the Evil Knievel. It has the same **Base** and many would call it a direct variation. I'm teaching the two separately because you'll most likely need to use The Fried Liver attack if your opponent is more experienced, or, if say, you've used The Evil Knievel so many times he figures it out.

I didn't come up with the name. This is what the Chess community actually calls it. There are different theories as to why it's called The Fried Liver Attack. I'd like to think it's because if it succeeds you win so much you fry your opponent's liver. The other theory is in England Fried Liver was a popular and well-liked dish at the time...kind've how a

Chipotle burrito is for me now. So the name of the opening is a comparison to the ease and popularity of Fried Liver.

FRIED LIVER ATTACK
POSITION #1: HE ATTACKS YOUR BISHOP WITH HIS QUEEN PAWN

If he notices you're up to something, his most likely action is to attack your Bishop and Pawn with his Queen Pawn like in the **image below.**

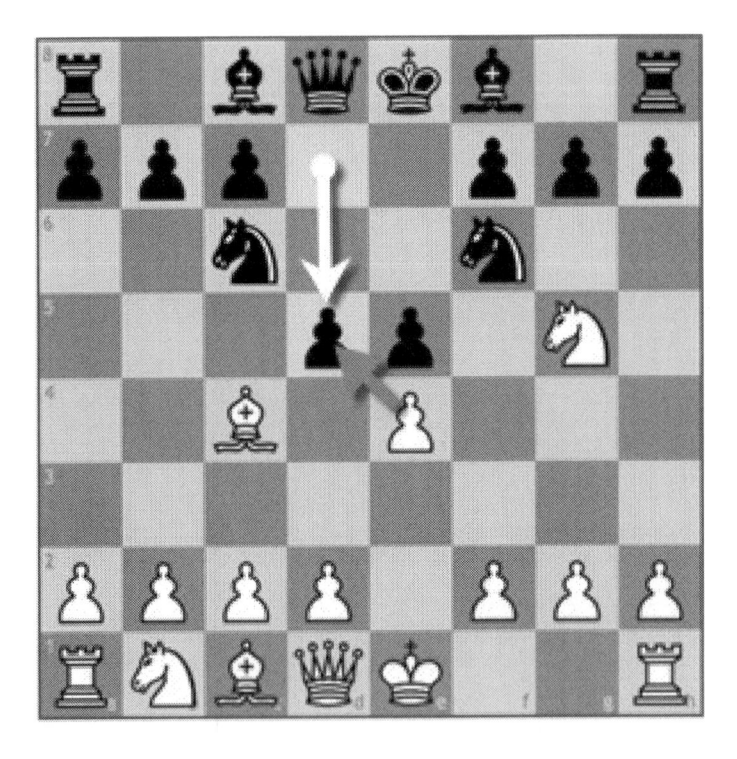

If he attacks your Bishop with Pawn to d5, you respond with **The Fried Liver Attack.**

FRIED LIVER ATTACK:
POSITION #2: YOU TAKE HIS PAWN WITH YOURS

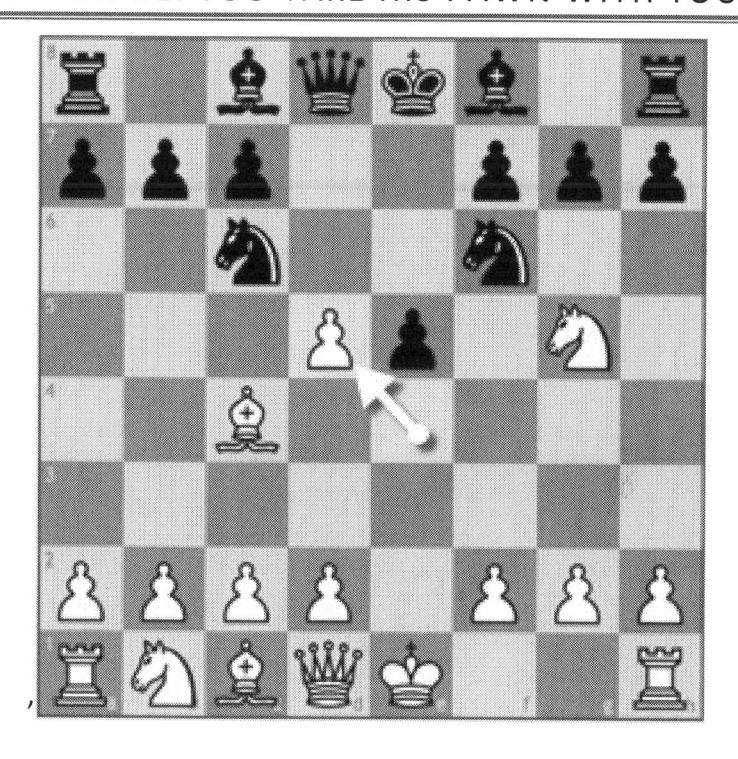

We take the Pawn, attacking his Knight.

FRIED LIVER ATTACK:
POSITION #3: HE TAKES YOUR PAWN WITH HIS KNIGHT

To protect his Knight, he takes your Pawn with his other Knight, successfully blocking your Bishop. Now he's thinking. "Ha*ha*. I foiled his plan. He can't take my Footman now. He won't be protected by his Bishop!" And, he's right. Your Knight won't be protected by your Bishop. But this is where you blow his mind...

FRIED LIVER ATTACK
POSITION #4: YOU TAKE HIS FOOTMAN ANYWAY

Even though you're not protected by the Bishop, you take the Footman anyway! What!? Yes. Because it forces the King to take your Knight, giving up his ability to Castle.

FRIED LIVER ATTACK
POSITION #5: HE TAKES YOUR KNIGHT

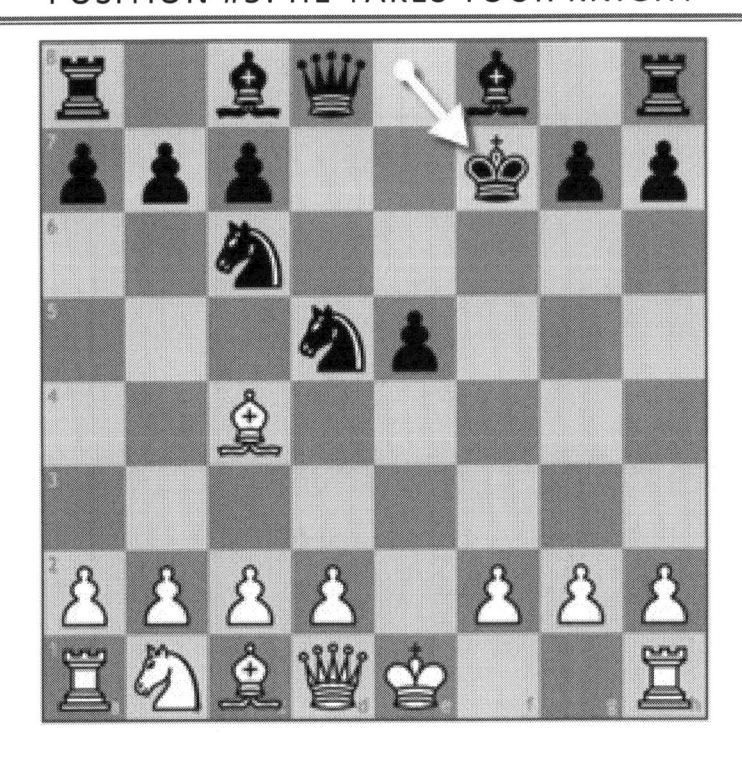

By taking your Knight, he's giving up any chance of Castling, putting his King into an extremely vulnerable position. Not only can he not castle, he's one Rank closer to your pieces. Did you give up your Knight for free? Yes, and that's the daredevil part. But you have a trick up your sleeve….

FRIED LIVER ATTACK
POSITION #4: YOU MOVE YOUR QUEEN TO F3.

Boom! Your Queen now has an open line to his uncastleable King. You're in a pretty sweet position from here. Your Bishop on c4 is pinning Black's Knight to the King and since your Queen is also attacking that Knight, you can easily take that piece if Black isn't paying attention.

You're now chasing his King across the board and Checkmate isn't far behind.

FRIED LIVER ATTACK CONCLUSION

While there's more to the Fried Liver Attack, you should have a pretty good idea of how it works now. It's not always going to go the way I show you here, which is when you're going to have to rely on good old-fashioned tactics and principles or variations, but I'm confident you can do it.

The main thing to take away from this Chapter is you can exploit the Footman (f7) Pawn by aligning your Knight and your Rook. Even if you sacrifice one of your pieces you force your opponent into a terrible position that will mean you win.

If you think you'll use the Evil Knievel or Fried Liver Attack as your opening, I highly recommend you check out this video from thechesswebsite.com. This video shows you the variations and how to checkmate from this point on:

Chess Openings: Fried Liver Attack
http://www.thechesswebsite.com/fried-liver-attack/

Here are some other classic Chess Openings with the same Base, you may be interested in.

Lolli Attack
http://youtu.be/ZmF64w13ZU8

Giuoco Piano
http://www.thechesswebsite.com/giuoco-piano/

THE KAMIKAZE MATE

THE KAMIKAZE MATE (THE 4-MOVE CHECKMATE)

The Chess community calls this **The Scholar's Mate,** but I call it the Kamikaze Mate because you're going to win or you're going to die trying. This is the Opening my student Eduardo used until I taught him **The Evil Knievel.**

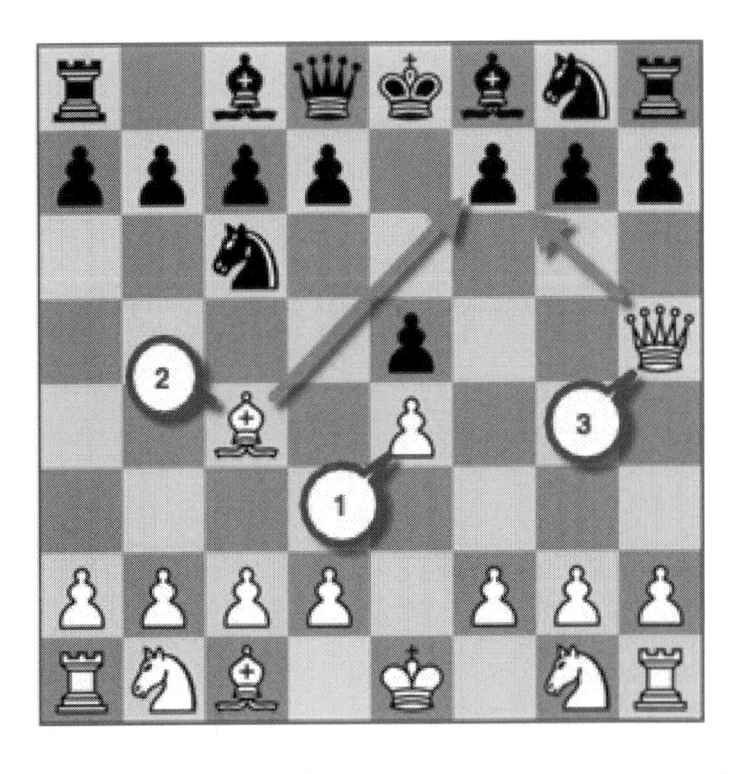

Here's how it works. Instead of developing the Knight first like the Evil Knievel, you attack the Footman Pawn with your Bishop right away. **(The numbers in the image above tell you which order to move the pieces.)** If your opponent doesn't defend appropriately, you take the Footman Pawn with your Queen. Checkmate.

Your opponent can't take the Queen with the King because it's protected by the Bishop.

250

Easy right? Here's what you need to know about this Opening. It's very risky for you because it pulls your Queen out right away. If your opponent manages to defend against it, you don't stand much chance of winning. But since we're talking about **beating your friends** (who probably know no strategy) it can be highly effective. In all reality, Eduardo probably won 100 games against his peers before I routinely shut this opening down and he changed it.

But if it works, your friends will think you're a total daredevil genius.

THE SPANISH BERZERKER

THE SPANISH BERZERKER

Here's an opening I used for a long time before I started using The Evil Knievel. I call it The Spanish Berzerker, but the Chess community would call it **The Ruy Lopez.** In terms of the first three moves, it's very similar to the Evil Knievel with one major difference. Your Bishop attacks his Knight instead of the Footman Pawn.

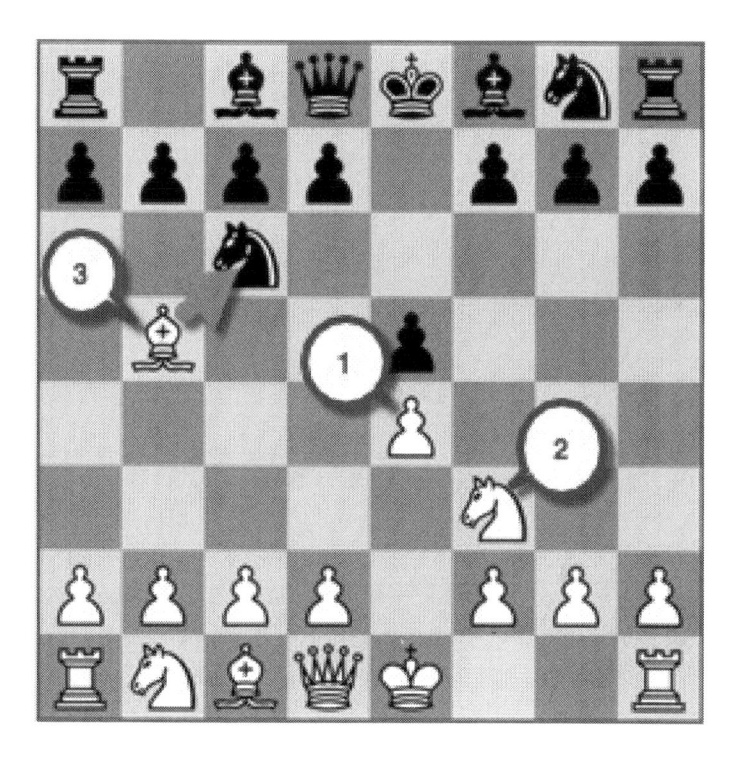

Here's why it's a daredevil opening, your next move is to sacrifice your Bishop for Black's Knight. Afterwards, it usually looks like this:

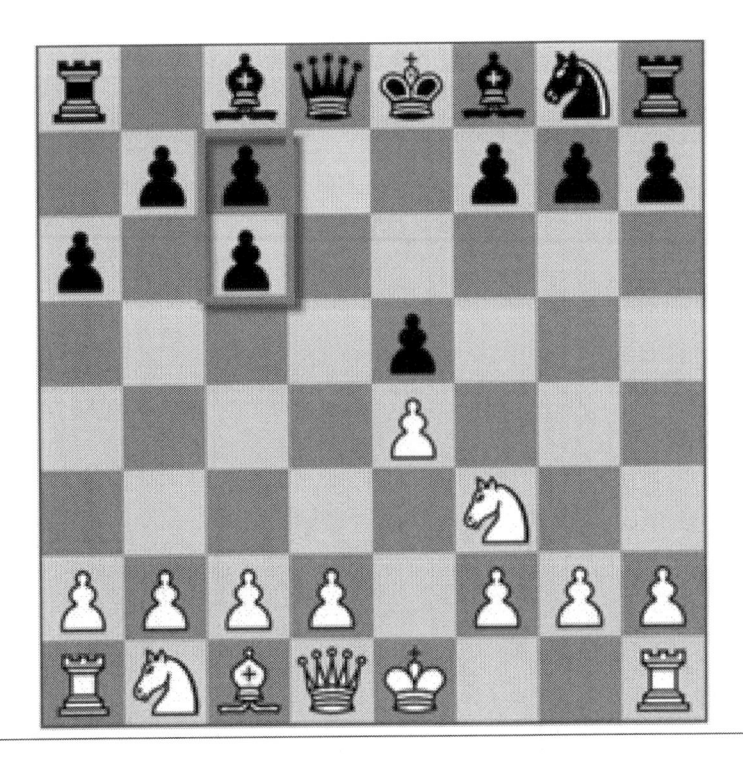

In the **image above,** Black attacked your Bishop with the Rook Pawn. But this was part of the plan. You sacrifice your Bishop for Black's Knight and your opponent ends up with doubled Pawns **(highlighted above).** Doubled Pawns are bad for your opponent because they lose the ability to protect each other. So, the **Payoff** in this opening is forcing your opponent to double his Pawns.

What makes this Opening a daredevil Opening is sacrificing your Bishop. Most beginners are afraid to sacrifice pieces.

It's not as daring or as bold as the The Evil Knievel or the Fried Liver Attack, but it's a great opening I've used many times.

BLACK OPENINGS

As Black you're always responding to White since White starts out a move ahead. So, it's really the best use of your time to learn White openings. But it is useful to know Black Openings as well. Here's the Black Opening I use almost exclusively.

THE FRENCH DEFENSE

In the **image above**, you see **The French Defense**. Simple, right? As Black, this is my favorite opening. Remember how we talked about how the **f7** Square is the weakest square on the board. The French Defense works because it protects the f7 Square right out of the gate. Let's just take a look if someone tried to pull the Evil Knievel on me:

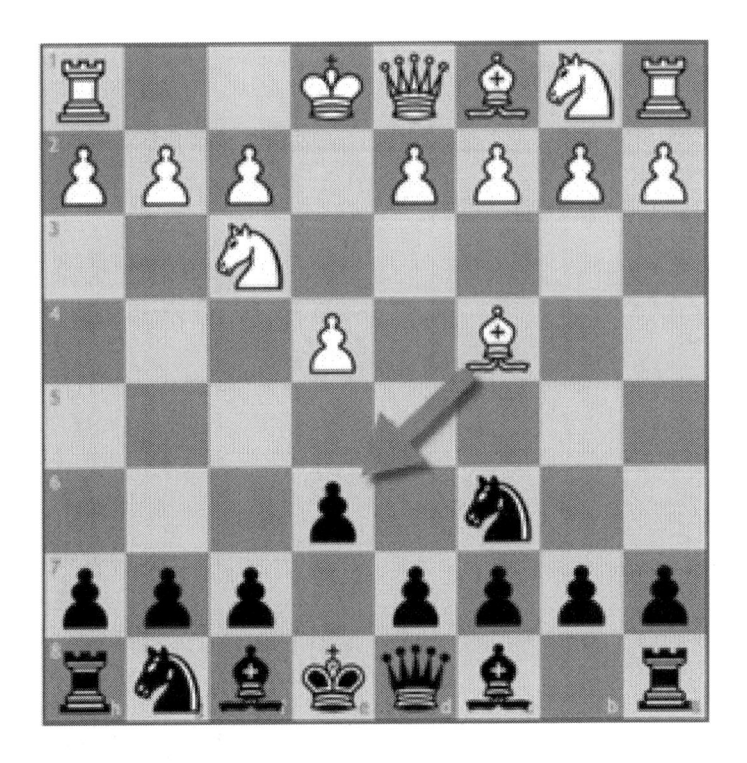

Nope. White's Bishop isn't getting through anytime soon. So that's not much of a threat. The Fried Liver Attack isn't likely to work either since my Queen is protecting the g5 square and my other Knight is protecting the e5 square. From that point, I usually try to reverse the Evil Knievel and attack White's f2 Pawn. Which would look like this:

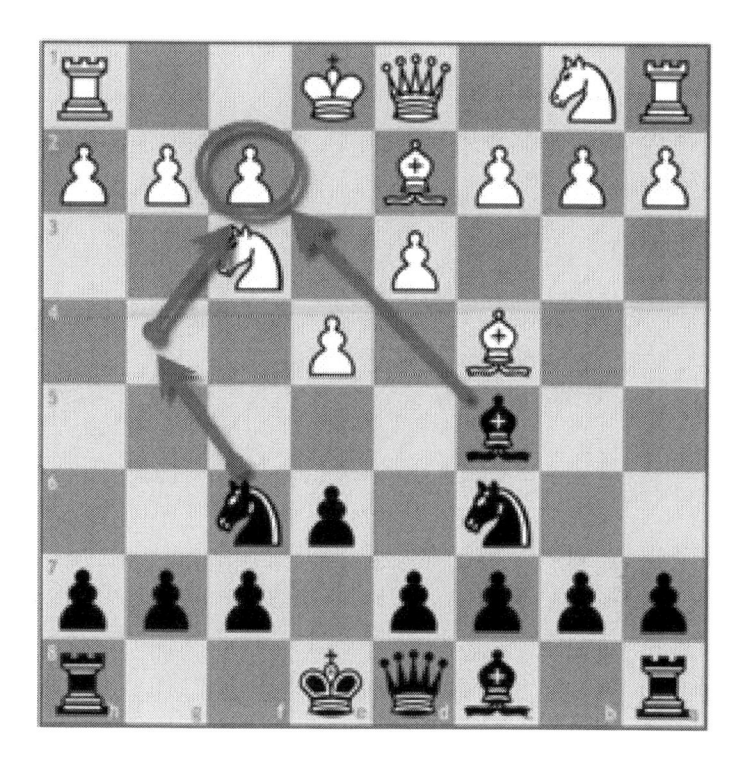

To summarize, the advantage of this Opening is that it shuts down The Evil Knievel, The Fried Liver, and The Kamikaze Mate and provides room for my Kingside Bishop and Queen to develop. On the downside, it doesn't grab for the center as well as it could. But you can easily adapt it for center control as well.

CHAPTER 6: OPENINGS...BRINGING IT ALL TOGETHER

CHAPTER 6: OPENINGS...BRINGING IT ALL TOGETHER

There they are. The most deadly and dangerous openings you can use to defeat your friends. But where do you go from here?

If your friends are reasonably good at Chess and you want a long-term Opening you can use for years to come, I highly recommend **The Evil Knievel** and **The Fried Liver Attack.** Start with these and you'll have a good foundation for many other openings.

If your friends are completely oblivious to Chess, learn **The Kamikaze Mate** (4-Move Checkmate) and start exploring ways you can adapt if you're not able to checkmate. I've seen people use it to great success against beginner players, but if you are serious about becoming good at Chess it won't win against better players.

If you're not quite ready for a high-risk opening, or you're good at middle game and tactics, I recommend **The Spanish Berzerker**.

LEARNING OPENINGS: STEP-BY-STEP

If you started learning Openings right now, what steps would you take?

1. Find your Opening

First, find an Opening you like. Go back and re-read the openings in this book and find one that seems appealing. Even though I highly recommend these openings for casual players and post-beginners, you may want to find your own Opening. Check out the openings at thechesswebsite.com.

Narrow it to down to a few, then go to Chess.com and try different openings on Live Chess. You may want to play unrated games to start since the point is to learn something new. Find the Opening that feels the best and stick with it.

2. Repeat and Memorize

Once you've decided on an opening, memorize the **Base** of the Opening. I would even recommend you use the video links I provide to learn the **Climax** and **Payoff** of your opening as well.

3. Practice and Problem Solve

Once you learn the opening, go online to Chess.com and play Live Chess and use that opening at least 20 times before learning another one. Get to know the ins and outs. Learn the variations. Remember the advantage of having your own Opening is you know it better than your opponent. If your opponent defeats your opening, find a way to stop it and improve it the next game.

OTHER OPENING TIPS.

Play your Opening as Fast Possible

If you play with a clock or you play online, you want to make your opening moves as fast as possible. One of the major advantages of knowing an opening is that you have it memorized. You can save yourself critical time later in the game by making the moves you know are good moves at the beginning.

Learn an Alternate Opening

Once you know your Opening like the back of your hand, learn an alternate Opening. When I used to play once a week against my friend Mark, he eventually figured out my Opening and the best ways to stop it. In order to throw him off my trail I learned a new Opening that was slightly different and it took him a while to catch up again. By the time he learned that one, I switched back to my first Opening and he was behind again. Then, I learned a new one and it was the same deal.

Know your Opening Principles

I've mentioned this before, but just in case you didn't take it seriously...**know your Opening Principles.** Your Opening isn't always going to go according to plan. In fact, most of the time, it's not. Know your Opening principles well so you can adjust and respond when your opponent throws you a curve ball.

Learn more Openings

Once you have your Openings down, start learning other openings. Learn as many as you can. You want to at least be able to recognize them. Find their weaknesses and strengths so you can defend against them. I would also recommend that you learn a few traps of common openings.

If you like the Daredevil Opening idea, check out this video from my favorite website for Chess Openings:

Top 7 Aggressive Openings
https://youtu.be/Ib8XaRKCAfo

These are some other bold (but slightly more complicated) Openings you can consider daredevil openings.

CONCLUSION

There they are. 4 Daredevil Openings to help you conquer your friends. I hope you've enjoyed reading and learning as much as I've enjoyed discussing "dangerous" Chess moves. Now you know how to play Openings that give YOU an advantage against your friends. But where do you go from here?

First, join the community of renegade casual Chess players.

I'm offering FREE Chess books available exclusively to my subscribers as well as other skill hacking tips and tricks. Join the mailing list.

You can also stay in touch via social media. Like my Facebook page or for Twitter, follow me @SkillArtist

I am always finding new websites, books, apps, boards and resources for Chess. I'm keeping a running list of resources I recommend at www.theskillartistsguide.com/chess-resources.

Now, you might have an undeniable edge after reading this book, but hey, there's no reason you can't share these secrets. Now is your chance to take what you've learned and give back to the community. Show a younger sibling your techniques, encourage learning and progress, or teach a friend these daredevil openings

...at their own risk, of course.

(Pssst. Want more?)

Email: maxen@skillhackr.com

Facebook: facebook.com/theskillartistsguide

Twitter: @SkillArtist

Blog: www.theskillartistsguide.com

(Want *even* more?)

NOW AVAILABLE IN PAPERBACK!

Now available in paperback!

If you liked this book, you may enjoy the first in the Conquer your Friends series: Chess mastery takes years, but to beat your friends? All you need is 8 easy principles. No history. No notation. Improve your Chess game today!

Buy eBook or Paperback from Amazon

DOWNLOAD YOUR FREE EBOOK!

Your first 5 to 10 moves are the most critical moves in the entire game. In this book, I show you **6 moves NOT to make** in the Opening. By simply NOT making these moves you gain a huge edge on your opponents. Join the casual Chess revolution today! Enter your email to download and receive free book offers and updates! 20 pages.

Download here

CONQUER YOUR FRIENDS WITH 10 DEADLY CHECKMATES

BY MAXEN TARAFA

www.theskillartistsguide.com

Chess: Conquer your Friends with 10 Deadly Checkmates
Copyright © 2015 by Maxen Tarafa
All rights reserved. This book or any portion thereof
may not be reproduced or used in any manner whatsoever without the express written permission of the publisher except for the use of brief quotations in a book review.
www.theskillartistsguide.com

CONQUER YOUR FRIENDS WITH 10 DEADLY CHECKMATES

FOR BEGINNERS AND CASUAL PLAYERS

Checkmate #1: Rook-Rook Mate (Leap Frog Mate)
Checkmate #2: Queen-Bishop Mate
Checkmate #3: King-Queen Mate
Checkmate #4: Back Rank Mate
Checkmate #5: Triangle Back-Rank Mate
Checkmate #6: King-Rook Mate
Checkmate #7: The Sniper Mate
Checkmate #8: The Pawn-Pin Mate
Checkmate #9: 4-Move Checkmate
Checkmate #10: Other Miscellaneous Checkmates

CHAPTER 1: 10 DEADLY CHECKMATES...THE SKILL ARTIST WAY

My name is Maxen R. Tarafa, and I'm a Skill Artist. If you're looking for a encyclopedia of Chess theory or a history of Chess, you've come to the wrong place. But if you're looking for 10 easy ways to checkmate your friends with deadly skill and accuracy, welcome to my dojo.

In my first book, Conquer your Friends with 8 Easy Principles, I showed you 8 of the easiest and highest impact Chess principles to improve your game today. In this book, I'm giving you 10 of the highest-impact checkmates to help you seal the deal, hammer the nail in the coffin, drop the mic, bury the hatchet, or end the game using any euphemism you like.

When you're nearing the end of the game, you know you need to checkmate your opponent before he checkmates you. But checkmate isn't always easy to see and even if you're ahead in pieces and you know you will win, many post-beginners and casual players don't see the steps they need to deliver the final blow.

Many casual players simply give up on games they were destined to win. In timed games, knowing how to checkmate with a certain set of pieces can mean the difference between winning and losing.

In this book, I'm showing you the most frequently used checkmates and checkmate patterns you can use today. Trained players are usually instructed in checkmate patterns, but usually only use a quarter of them. You can learn how to finish the game 80 percent of the time using a few easy checkmates and checkmate patterns, which I'm going to show you in this book.

I'm giving you ten easy but powerful checkmates with clear situations where you can use them and pictures showing you exactly what to do. If you learn these checkmates and practice, I promise you will have yet another massive edge on your friends.

But remember, with great skills come great responsibility.

I trust you'll use them wisely.

Cordially,

Maxen R. Tarafa

CHAPTER 2: HOW TO LEARN FROM THIS BOOK

In this book, I'm showing you moves that deliver the final blow. Unlike most Chess books, in this book I use no notation and no complex terminology.

Basic Knowledge

To learn from this book, you only need a basic knowledge of Chess. What is basic knowledge? You should know how to:

1. Set up the board
2. Move each piece
3. Checkmate

The third item is important. You must understand the basics of checkmate. If you've ever won a game of Chess, I assume you already know how to checkmate. If you want to learn or refresh your knowledge of how to checkmate, you may want to check out my book for beginners: How to Play Chess for (Absolute) Beginners. Where there is a chapter dedicated to checkmate. A simple Google search will also suffice.

Max/Min Experience Level

This book is designed specifically for casual players and post-beginners. If you haven't formally trained in Chess, this book will most likely be perfect for you. If you have, this book is going to be most helpful for players who have just learned the basics up to a max rating level of around 1200 ELO. Remember this is for post-beginners to learn fast so they can move on with their lives, it's not an end-all be-all. If you're above a rating level 1200 ELO you're most likely going to be in

Snoozetown unless you want ideas for checkmates to teach to your students, kids, or younger siblings.

Images

When I'm explaining a Chess move or principle that I think needs an image, I'll show you something like the **following image**.

Instead of using notation, I use highlights and arrows to describe exactly what I'm talking about. Even though it's quite intuitive, it helps to know what each arrow means. If your device is in color, the arrows are Red or White. If your device is Black and White, they'll appear Dark Grey or White. Below is a key:

271

Red/Dark Grey Square – Highlights a key square or piece

Red/Dark Grey Arrow – Active Arrow – Shows where a piece is attacking or the active direction of the piece

White Arrow with a Dot – Shows where a piece came from in the previous move.

White Arrow without a Dot – Shows less active attacking activity

Board Orientation

You can always assume the bottom of the image represents your side of the board or the side closest to you. In this book, in most examples you are playing White. While the checkmates work for Black or White, in my experience post-beginners are most comfortable playing White. The point here is not to challenge the post-beginner's ability to play Black or White, but to learn 10 easy checkmates.

Engage your Senses

As you read, you may want to play with a Chessboard next to you (especially if you're a kinesthetic learner). Or with a Chess Program (such as Chess.com) open in a separate window. It will help to practice the principles as you go.

Alright, housekeeping is done. Let's move on to some basic facts about checkmate to get us in the mood.

CHECKMATE FACT SHEET

In the next chapter, I'm going to give you ten easy checkmates, but first I'm going to give you a cheat sheet of checkmate facts that can help you lay your opponent down for the big sleep.

1. A Queen alone cannot checkmate.

A Queen with a **Helper Piece** can checkmate. A Queen and a King can checkmate. A Queen can checkmate when the opposing King is surrounded by his own pieces. But a Queen alone CANNOT checkmate.

2. The easiest place to checkmate is the corner

When the opposing King is in the corner of the board, it's much easier to checkmate. A corner naturally reduces the directions a King can escape.

3. The second easiest place to checkmate is the edge

Again, based on the idea that if a King has less directions to which he can escape, the edge is the second best place since there is one less direction for the King to go.

4. It's hardest to checkmate in the middle of the board

Word to the wise: If you have no pieces left except your King, the middle is usually the best place to be since it will be harder for your opponent to checkmate you.

5. The fastest checkmate is within two moves

Although it's rare, it is possible to checkmate within two moves. However, it depends more on your opponent making bad moves than you making good ones. A three move checkmate is also possible. The four move checkmate is called the Scholar's Mate and is often used by beginners. Although the Scholar's Mate does not work well against experienced players, it can be effective against many less experienced post-beginners and casual players. We will discuss it in this book mainly (ahem) for defensive purposes.

6. More than 32 Checkmates have earned names

Some checkmates are given names by the Chess community either because of their frequency or because they are interesting for other reasons. Wikipedia lists thirty two of them and more exist. Some names include: The Lolli Mate, The Fool's Mate, David and Goliath Mate, and The Back Rank Mate.

While some are useful to learn, in this book we'll focus only on the most frequent and high-impact checkmates to get you the most checkmating power in the least amount of time.

KEY TERMS

In order to fully understand this book, you will need to understand a few key terms. For the most part, these terms are self-explanatory but it never hurts to get ahead of the game. If they don't make sense now, don't worry about it. I promise they will make sense when you see them in action later in the book.

Check and Checkmate

A refresher for people who are new. **Check** is when a piece attacks the King, but the King can escape or block the attack. **Checkmate** is when the King is under attack and cannot escape, block the attack, or capture the attacking piece within one move.

Containment (or contain)

To **Contain** is to prevent a King from moving to a certain square, an entire Rank or File (Row or Column), or side of the board. The purpose is not to attack the King, but to prevent him from escaping a certain boundary.

Helper Piece

Since no piece alone, not even a Queen, can deliver checkmate by itself. You need to have a second piece to help you checkmate. The **Helper Piece** serves one of three functions. 1) It **Contains** the King while another piece delivers checkmate. 2) It **Protects** the piece that delivers checkmate or 3) It **Smothers** the King by physically sitting on a square the King would escape to. The Helper Piece is usually one of your pieces, but it doesn't have to be. In the case of a Back Rank Mate or a Smothered Mate, your opponent's pieces can serve as a Helper Piece by **Smothering** their own King.

Rank

A Rank is simply a row on the Chess board. You may have heard this term from the famous checkmate called a Back Rank Mate.

Let's Checkmate!

Knowledge is power. But checkmates are everything (when it comes to Chess anyway) so without further ado, let's learn 10 deadly checkmates.

CHECKMATE #1: THE ROOK-ROOK MATE

One of the most common but absolutely critical checkmates is with two Rooks. In this checkmate, I'm going to show you how to use a technique (or checkmating pattern) I call the **Leap Frog Technique**. Some people also call it the **Ladder Technique**. The Leap Frog Technique is important to learn because you can also apply the **Leap Frog** technique to two Queens or a Rook and a Queen.

How to Begin The Rook-Rook Mate

In the **image above**, you're playing White. You have two rooks and as long as you don't make any major blunders, you're going to win. But you're going to need a little technique if you don't want it to take forever.

Your first step is to **Contain** the opposing King. Notice how the Rook in the **image above** is not checking or attacking the Black King. It simply blocks the Black King off from one half of the board. Once the King is contained, our next objective is to push the Black King to the top edge of the board using the **Leap Frog technique**.

278

Now that you're certain the King cannot move to the bottom of the board, you move your other Rook one square beyond the previous Rook and check the King. Do you see how this is similar to the children's game Leap Frog? Each Rook "leaps" over beyond the previous Rook. You will continue this pattern: moving each Rook one square beyond the previous one until the King reaches the top edge.

Notice the King can't move down the board because the bottom Rook prevents him from moving downward. From here, it's a simple game of leapfrog. While one Rook contains, the other checks the King, forcing him rank by rank to the top of the board.

Next, you move your first Rook one rank beyond the other rook. Are you seeing a pattern here? Notice the Black King must move up.

Continuing the Leap Frog motion. After this, there is only one file left to attack.

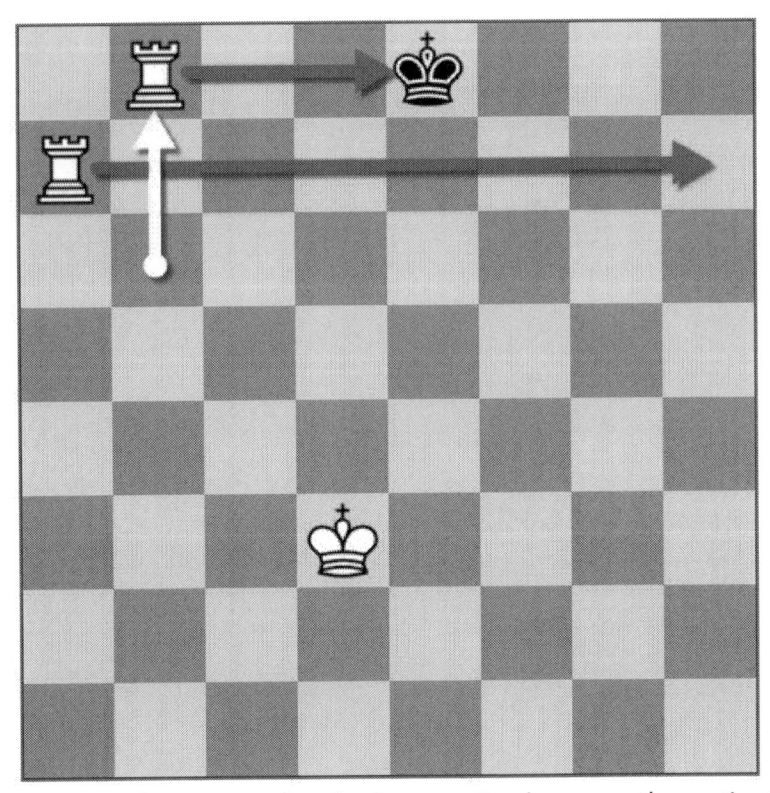

And finally, checkmate. Notice the bottom Rook covers the entire 7th rank preventing any means of escape. While the first Rook, moves to the back rank, delivering checkmate. Booyah.

CHECKMATE #2:
QUEEN-BISHOP MATE (UP CLOSE AND PERSONAL TECHNIQUE)

In this checkmate, you're using your Queen and a **helper piece** to get **Up Close and Personal** with the opponent's King. Observe the **image above** to see how the final checkmate position will look. While I use a Bishop in this example, this checkmate can be performed with a Queen and any other piece.

You'll need a few ingredients to make this checkmate possible.

First, the enemy King needs to be on the edge of the board. You can use the **Leap Frog technique** above or the **Knight Shadow technique** (shown later) to move your opponent to the edge of the board. By forcing to the King to the edge of the board, you're reducing the number of squares to which he can escape. This will make checkmate ten times easier than trying to checkmate in the center of the board.

Second, you're going to need a **helper piece**. In the **image above** the Bishop acts as the helper piece in the checkmate.

Third, both pieces need to be covering the square opposite of the edge the board from the King. Do you see where the attack lines from the King and Queen intersect? By safely placing your Queen on that intersection you will checkmate every time. I call this getting **Up Close and Personal.** See the **image below** for how it looks.

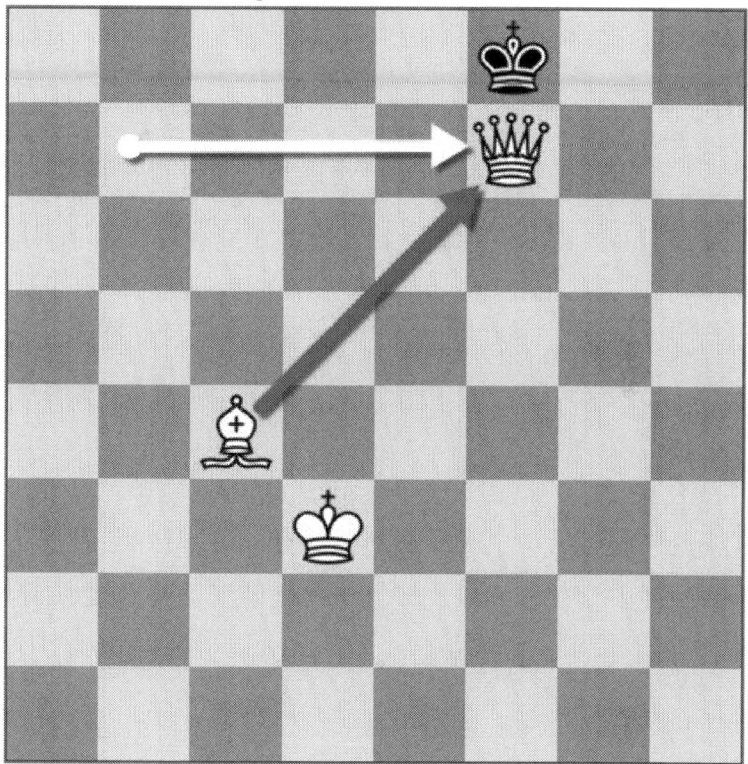

In the **image above**, the White Queen moves to the square opposite the edge of the board. Notice how the King cannot take the Queen because the helper piece, the Bishop, is protecting the Queen. The King cannot move to any nearby squares because the Queen attacks them.

This checkmate is possible with any two pieces and anywhere on the board as long as you have the ingredients mentioned above. To review, you'll need to make sure:

1. The King is on the edge of the board
2. You have a helper piece
3. Your helper and your Queen intersect opposite the edge of the board

The **image above** shows the Knight protecting the square opposite the edge, allowing the Queen to get **Up close and Personal.**

Even the Pawn can be the helper piece.

287

The enemy King doesn't have to be on the top edge of the board. For example, in the **image above**, the King is on left edge of the board, but the **Up Close and Personal Mate** still works because the helper piece (the Bishop) protects the square opposite of the left edge of the board and the Queen is on it.

CHECKMATE #3:
KING-QUEEN MATE (KNIGHT SHADOW TECHNIQUE)

The King and Queen Mate is more difficult than other mates, but it is critical that the post-beginner learn it. It's important to learn because if you don't know the technique, checkmate can literally take hours. Even though theoretically it's a guaranteed win, many beginners give up on this mate simply because they don't know how to do it. So, let me save hours of your life and possible loss of games by showing it to you now.

In the **image above** you are playing White. Your objective is to force the Black King into the corner and checkmate. However, this is no small task. If you move your Queen too close, you allow the King to escape the clutches of your Queen, resulting in perpetual fumbling around in the middle of the board.

You want to move your Queen to a place where 1) You contain the enemy King, and 2) You force him to the move to the corner you want him to (in this case the upper right corner of the board).

In order to accomplish this, you will need to use the **Knight's Shadow Technique**. What is a Knight's shadow? In the **image above**, the Queen is a Knight's shadow from the Black King. The gray arrow shows a Knight's shadow. If you imagined the Queen was a Knight, it would be attacking the King. Of course, she's not attacking the King, but being in this position allows the White Queen to be **close enough to contain, but far enough not to be captured.**

In the next phase, the White Queen mirrors the Black King's moves. If the King moves right, the White Queen moves one square right. If the Black King moves up, the White Queen moves one square up. See the pattern? In the **image above**, the Black King is moving one square right, and the White Queen is also following one square right.

The Black King moves one square diagonal-up. The White Queen follows one square diagonal-up.

Finally, the Black King moves diagonal-left. But this is where you STOP.

THIS IS EXTREMELY IMPORTANT. If you move any further, the Queen may stalemate the Black King. The Black King must have at least two safe squares to move to.

Okay, you know not to stalemate the Black King. But what's next?

Next, you're going to get your King involved.

Now you're going to move your King toward the Black King. Notice the Black King can move back and forth in the two squares along the top of the board.

In the interest of saving time for you and trees for the rainforest (or batteries on your device), I've skipped to where your King gets close to the Black King. What you should notice about the **image above** is the Black King cannot move any closer to the Black King. Your next step is to get Up Close and Personal with the Queen, using your King as the helper piece.

Boom. See the **image above**. You get your Queen Up Close and Personal and checkmate.

Let's review.

First, you forced the King into the corner using the **Knight's Shadow Technique**. Then you moved your King close enough to use as a helper piece. To deliver the final blow, you got your Queen Up Close and Personal.

The keys to this checkmate are 1) Using the Knight's Shadow Technique, 2) remembering NOT TO STALEMATE, and 3) using your King as a helper piece. As long as you remember those three things and you don't get your Queen captured. Checkmate is yours for the taking.

CHECKMATE #4:
THE BACK RANK MATE

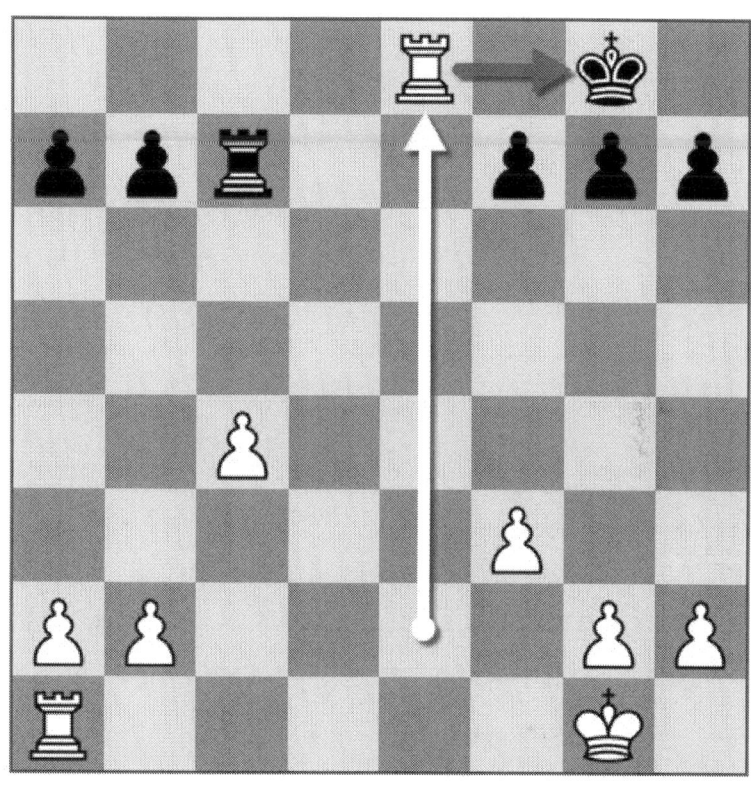

Ahhh, the famous Back Rank Mate. I showed this crucial checkmate in my first book Chess: Conquer your Friends with 8 Easy Principles. But, I'm showing it again for two reasons. One, it's perhaps, the easiest and most frequent checkmate you can possibly get. Second, I'm going to expand on the Back Rank and show you other similar checkmates based on the Back Rank mate, so if you don't know this one yet, pay close attention.

Before I show you how it works, you may be able to recognize it on your own. In the **image above**, White can checkmate in one move. Can you find the one move that will result in checkmate?

298

If you didn't find it, don't worry. In two pages you're going to know exactly how it works.

The first thing you're looking for in a Back Rank mate is a wall formed by three Pawns in front of your opponent's King (highlighted above). In the **image above**, notice the King is on the back row (a row is also called a Rank in Chess terms). Also notice there are no other pieces protecting that row. The only piece that's close is the Black Rook, but since it's not on the back rank, you can mate in one move.

A wall of Pawns protecting the King is typically good since the Pawns protect the King from enemy attacks. But in this case, they are also smothering the King so that if another piece can attack the entire Back

Rank, that King has nowhere to escape. And what piece does White have that can attack the entire Back Rank?

Yes, the White Rook. See the **image above**. Notice in one move the White Rook can move to the back rank and checkmate. And another one bites the dust!

If the Black King had even one square to escape to, the game would go on. But there is no square for the Black King to escape. Black's own Pawns, the pieces meant to protect him, also smother him and make checkmate a piece of cake. That's the beauty of the Back Rank! Simply recognizing this weakness can end a game long before it should, giving you mind-blowing checkmate power.

CHECKMATE #5: TRIANGLE BACK RANK MATE

Of course, it would be great if all checkmates were as easy as the Back Rank. Unfortunately, they're not. Luckily, you can apply the Back Rank principle to other checkmates to make them almost as easy. In the **image above**, we have a similar set-up, but this time, Black has predicted the Back Rank Mate and moved his middle Pawn up one square to give his King a place to escape. See the **image above**.

Now, many players would think "shoot, I lost my chance for the Back-Rank mate." But, let's not throw the baby out with the bathwater. If you can attack the square where the King *would* escape, you can still attack the Back Rank with your Rook and it will still be checkmate.

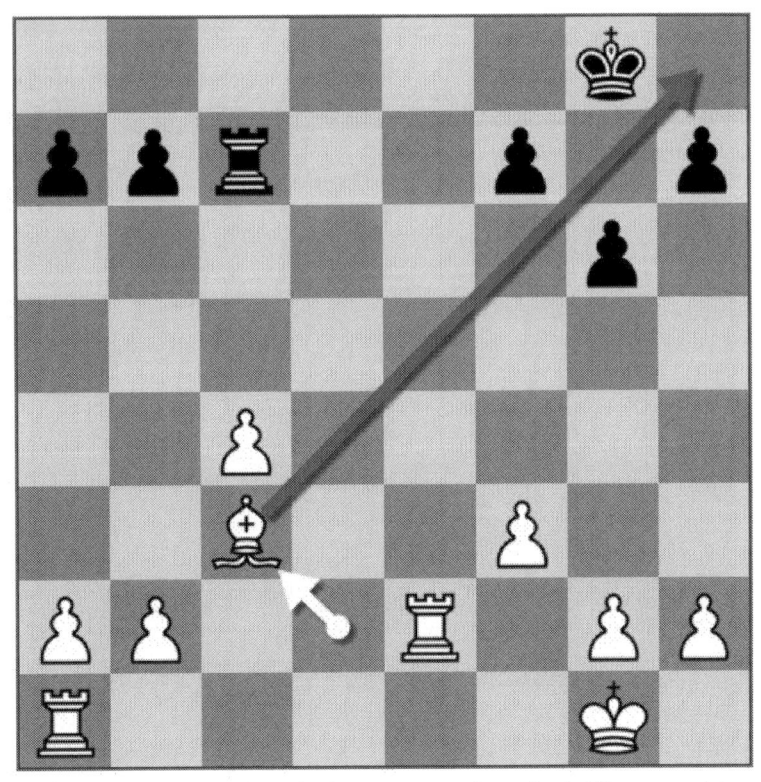

In the **image above**, we attack the square the Black King would escape to. Now, you may be thinking, but If I do that, he'll move another Pawn up and give himself another square to escape!

You may be right. If your opponent has his wits about him, he may take defensive action. But, if your opponent is a casual player or post-beginner there's a good chance they won't even notice. It's hard enough for them to notice they're at risk of being Back-Ranked, and it's even harder for them to notice their escape square is under attack.

Okay, now you're preventing any possibility of escape. Can you guess what's next?

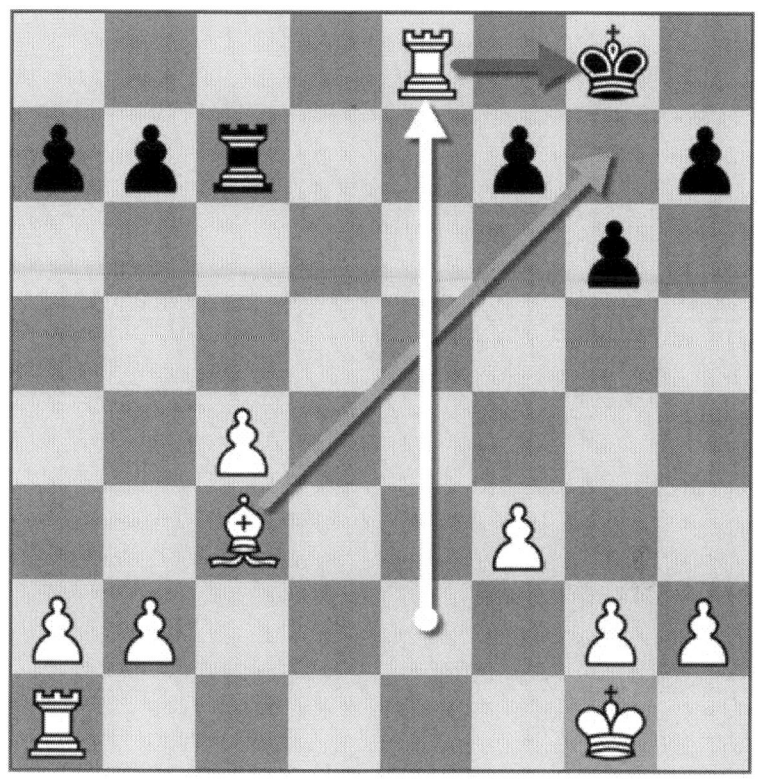

Right. You move your Rook up to the Back Rank to checkmate the King, just like the Back Rank mate. See the **image above**. Notice the Black King cannot move into his little Pawn triangle because the White Bishop is already attacking it.

That's how you use the Back Rank Principle to achieve a checkmate without it actually being a Back Rank Mate.

CHECKMATE #6:
KING-ROOK MATE

In this checkmate, we're going to use the Back Rank principle to checkmate again. But this time, the signals that the Back Rank is imminent are not as obvious.

In the **image above**, you're playing White. it appears as if the Black King has plenty of space since the only piece close to him is White's measly King. To the untrained eye, this may not seem like a threat. However, if you know what you're looking for, you'll notice that White can checkmate using the Back Rank principle in one move.

In the **image above**, you see the squares the King is attacking. Notice anything familiar? The King creates the same three-square wall that Black's Pawns created in the original Back Rank mate. All one needs to do is move a piece to the Back Rank that can cover the entire Back Rank in one move.

305

Boom. This is a common checkmate that post-beginners need to know. Sometimes it won't be as easy as back ranking the opposing King. First, the King needs to be on the back rank, but luckily, you already know two similar techniques to get him there. One is the **Leap Frog Technique**. The other is the **Knight Shadow Technique**. You will need to use both pieces to wrangle that King into the corner, but once he's there, checkmate is easy as two words: Back Rank.

CHECKMATE #7: QUEEN-BISHOP MATE (SNIPER MATE)

If your opponent is experienced and protects his Bank Rank or simply disallows you from back-ranking him, you're going to have to break through the fortress made of his Pawns after he has castled. This can be a daunting task. In this checkmate and the next few checkmates following, I'm going to show you a few methods to break through the fortress. The techniques used to accomplish these checkmates come from a few of the checkmates we've already learned. You will be getting Up Close and Personal and even recognizing the same Pawn structures as the Back Rank Mate.

307

In the **image above**, Black's Back Rank is protected by a Rook, preventing a quick and easy Back Rank Mate. However, you can use what I call the sniper method to break through Black's fortress.

To use the sniper method, you need a **Helper Piece** (in this case, the Bishop) and a Queen. Black got into this position by castling. Castling has many advantages, one of which is hiding himself behind a wall of protective Pawns. However, one disadvantage is the King's position on the edge of the board: A disadvantage we are going to exploit.

In the **image above**, notice how both the Bishop and the Queen are pointing to the center Pawn. To Black, it may appear that he is protected by his wall of Pawns. But we know better. As long as we are protected by a helper piece, not only can we take the Pawn in front of the King, we can also checkmate the Black King.

In the next move, the White Queen takes the center Pawn. Checkmate. The King cannot take the Queen because she is protected by the White Bishop. And he has nowhere to escape since the Queen is attacking all available squares. If this checkmate looks exactly like the Bishop-Queen Mate, it's because it *is* the same. The only difference is you're breaking through the wall of Pawns in front of the Black King. Otherwise, it's the same mate.

It's important to notice this same checkmate can apply to other Pawn configurations.

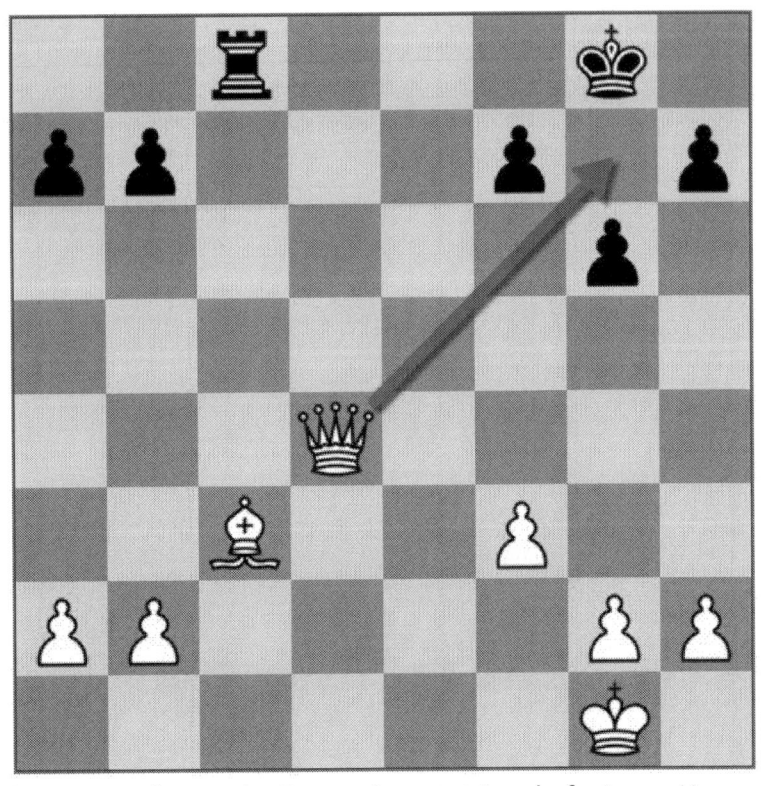

In the **image above**, the Pawns form a triangle fortress. However, checkmate is still one move away.

This is another common configuration, but still mate is one move away.

CHECKMATE #8:
THE PAWN-PIN MATE

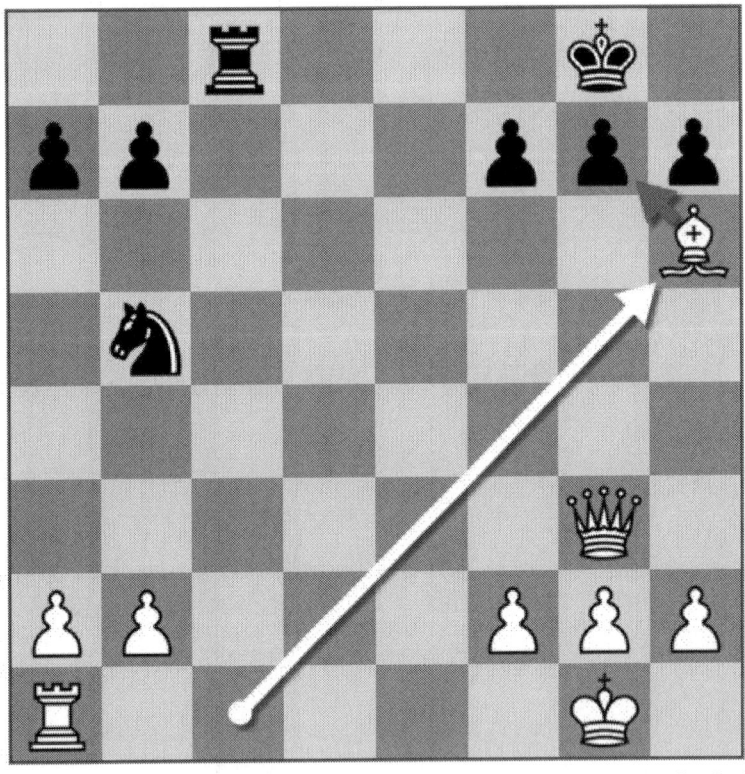

This mate will require you to use chess tactics or a "weapon" of Chess. If you read *8 Easy Principles*, you will know how to use a Pin. This is yet another way to break through the fortress. As you will see, it works by Pinning the middle Pawn to the King.

312

The first step in the Pawn-Pin mate is to move your Queen between the center Pawn, (or any other Pawn in front of the King). Your opponent likely won't notice, but that Pawn is now pinned to the King (meaning the Pawn cannot move out of the way since exposing your own King to checkmate is illegal). Now that the Pawn is pinned, what are we going to do about it? We're going to exploit it, of course!

In the **image above**, we've moved the Bishop right into attacking position of the center Pawn. At this point, your opponent probably thinks you're insane! Normally, this would be suicide for our Bishop. But, since the Pawn is pinned by the Queen, it cannot take our Bishop. Now, Black *can* take defensive action at this point, but often post-beginners and casual players don't recognize the danger they're in. And if they don't, you make the following move...

Boom. Checkmate. You pull another Up Close and Personal Mate like it's nobody's business. It's important to know this checkmate works with similar Pawn configurations.

In the **configuration above**, the edge Pawn is moved up. Again, it would normally be suicide for the Bishop to take the Pawn as indicated in the **image above**, but since we know the Pawn that protects it is Pinned by the Queen, it's a free meal for our Bishop and very likely checkmate.

In general, checkmates won't always work the way you want. However, setting up a checkmate that doesn't work can be useful because it forces your opponent to respond to your game.

CHECKMATE #9:
THE KAMIKAZE MATE (4-MOVE CHECKMATE)

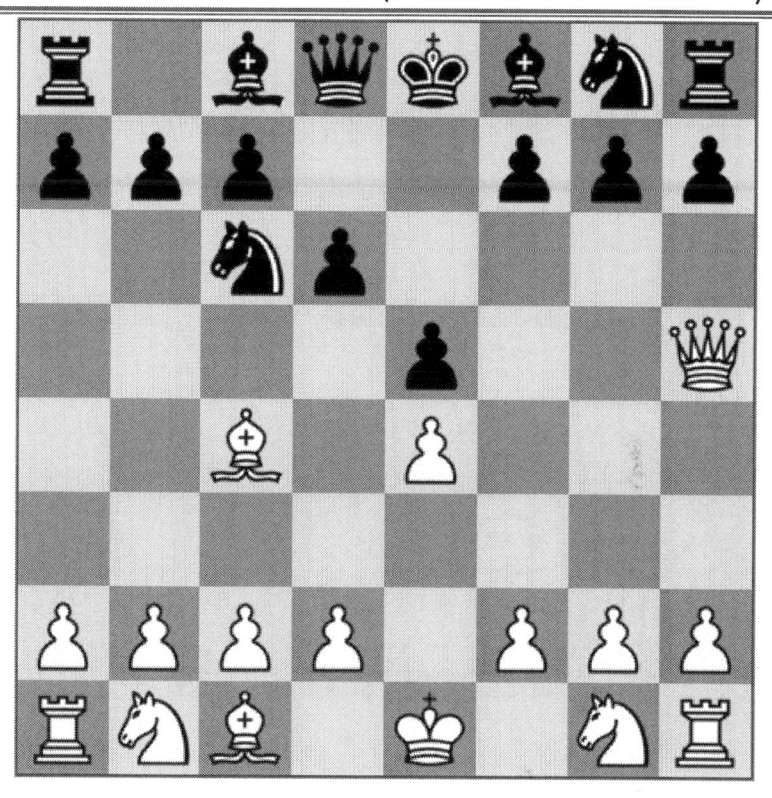

This is an Opening/Checkmate hybrid everyone should know—if not for the embarrassment-inducing power of it, then for defensive purposes. In this checkmate, your Queen will break through Black's Pawn structure, and get Up Close and Personal with Black's King and three other major pieces.

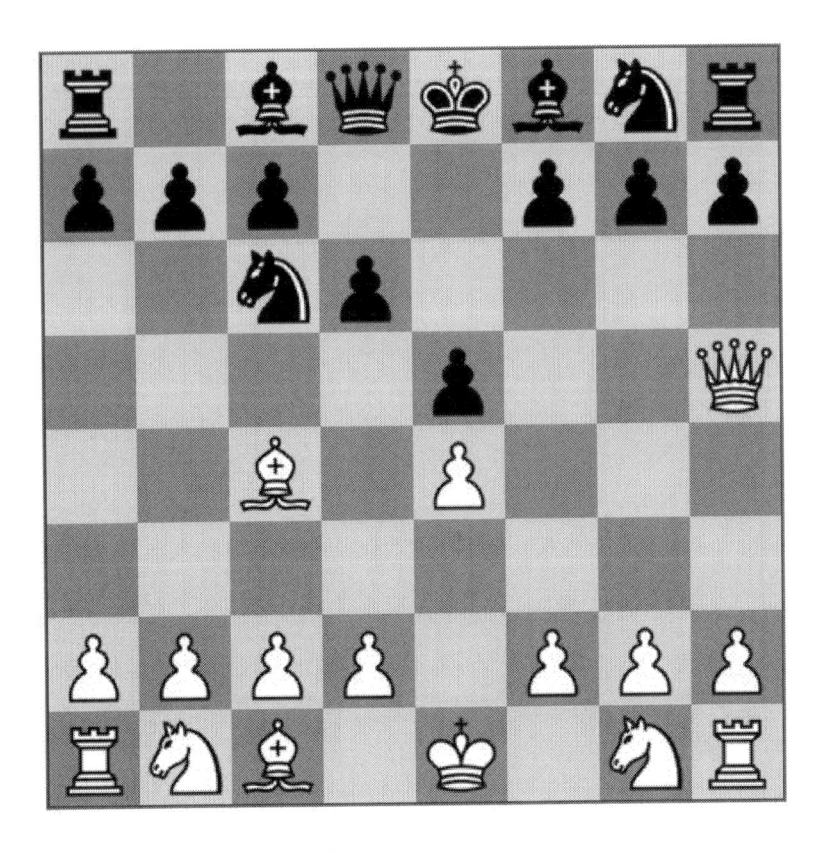

In the **image above**, you see the set-up for the 4-move Kamikaze Mate. You're playing White. Can you find checkmate in one move using the Bishop as a helper?

That's right. Move the Queen to the infamous f7 square and it's checkmate. No pieces can attack the Queen and there's nowhere for Black's King to escape. If you're interested in this opening, I explain it in more detail in my book, Chess: Conquer your Friends with 4 Daredevil Openings.

While most chess players figure out how to stop this opening/checkmate quickly, knowing this opening can be good training for checkmating early and openings in general. It serves as a reminder that checkmates aren't only for the end of the game, you can also checkmate in the opening and the middle game if the right elements are in place.

CHECKMATE #10: OTHER MISCELLANOUS CHECKMATES

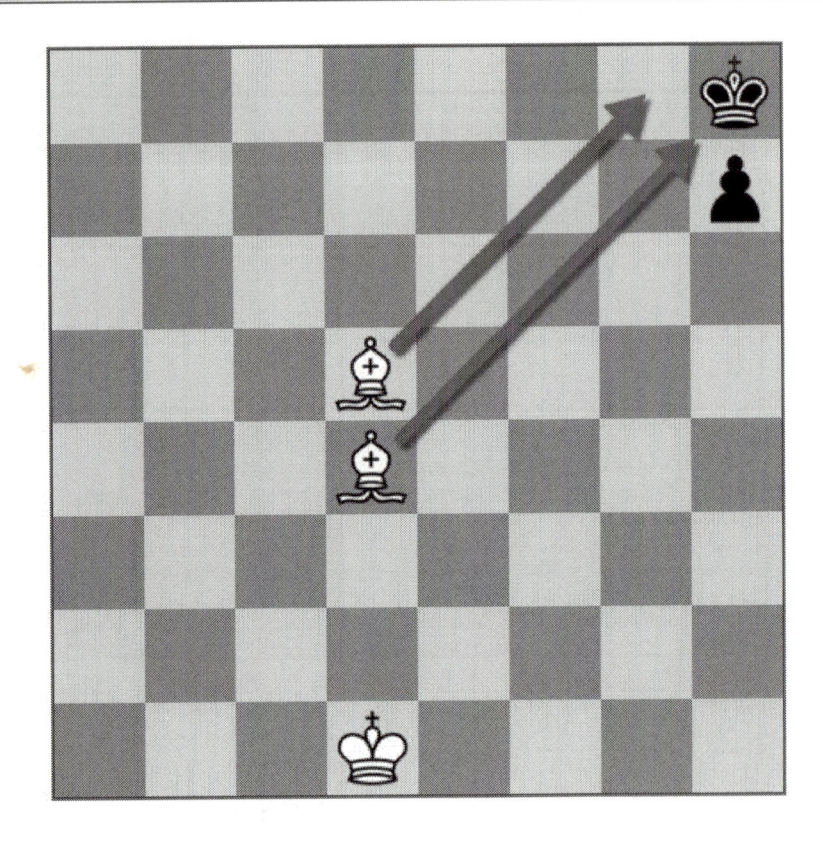

While I've shown you what I believe to be the easiest and highest-impact checkmates in the game, there are so many more I wanted to include in the book, but they didn't quite make the top ten. I'm going to show you a sampling of some other helpful checkmates you may want to know.

Bishop-Bishop Mate

In the **image above**, you see the Bishop-Bishop mate. The key to this checkmate is forcing the King into a corner by using your two-Bishops like the Rooks in the **Leap Frog Technique**. In this image, the Bishops are helped by the Pawn in front of the King. If you're not lucky enough to have a Pawn helping you, you will need to use your King to help contain the opposing King. See the **image below**.

Knight and Bishop Mate

This is a hard, but frequently occurring checkmate. Again, you must move the King into the corner with your King helping. The Knight will cover the surrounding squares and your Bishop will deliver the final blow. The exact positions of these pieces is less important than the basic configuration.

Rook-Bishop Mate

This checkmate uses the Rook to contain the King, isolating him to one possible space while another piece delivers the checkmating blow (the Bishop). See the **image above**. This is an important pattern to remember since the helper in this situation is not protecting the blow-delivering piece, but simply keeps the King in place.

In this situation, however, it's important to keep an eye on stalemate. Anytime you force the King into a place he cannot move to any other squares, you are risking a stalemate. It works in this situation, however, because Black still has two Pawns he could potentially move, preventing any chance of stalemate.

Smothered Mate

What's interesting about this checkmate is that Black is surrounded by two of his most powerful pieces, and yet they are helpless to defend against checkmate. In the **image above**, you see White's Knight delivering the final blow. If Black had an extra move, or even one space available to escape, Black would most likely win this game. However, as the name promises, Black is smothered by his own pieces.

CONCLUSION

Congratulations! You now know ten easy and high-impact checkmates to finish your friends in Chess. Now you can ride off into the sunset singing "Another One Bites the Dust." But where do you go from here?

If you're a casual player or post-beginner, I highly recommend you check out my first book: <u>Chess: Conquer your Friends with 8 Easy Principles</u>. You'll learn eight of the easiest, most high-impact principles to learn Chess fast.

If you're a go-getter and you've already read 8 Easy Principles, you may want to try <u>Chess: Conquer your Friends with 4 Daredevil Openings.</u> The opening is one of the most critical and overlooked techniques for casual players and post-beginners and if you don't have an opening yet or don't even know what an Opening is, this book is for you.

Now, you might have an undeniable edge after reading this book, but hey, there's no reason you can't share these secrets. Now is your chance to take what you've learned and give back to the community. Show a younger sibling your techniques, encourage learning and progress, or teach a friend these 10 easy checkmates.

...after they've begged for mercy, of course.

(Pssst. Want more?)

MORE WAYS TO CONQUER YOUR FRIENDS!

Now Available in eBook or Paperback!

CONQUER YOUR FRIENDS with 4 DAREDEVIL OPENINGS

CHESS

A Cheat Sheet for Casual Players and Post-Beginners

MAXEN TARAFA

You know you need to control the center, but exactly how do you do it? Answer: An Opening. Learn the exact moves to control the center, steal your opponent's pieces, and even checkmate your opponent with your first 5 moves.

Buy eBook or Paperback from Amazon

NOW AVAILABLE IN EBOOK OR PAPERBACK!

If you liked this book, you may enjoy the first in the Conquer your Friends series: Learn the most high-impact basic strategy. All you need is 8 easy principles. No history. No notation. Improve your Chess game today!

Buy eBook or Paperback from Amazon

Printed in Great Britain
by Amazon